RAND

Merging University Students into K–12 Science Education Reform

Valerie L. Williams

Prepared for the
National Science Foundation

Science and Technology Policy Institute

The research described in this report was conducted by RAND's Science and Technology Policy Institute for the National Science Foundation under contract ENG-9812731.

ISBN: 0-8330-3089-2

Published 2002 by RAND
1700 Main Street, P.O. Box 2138, Santa Monica, CA 90407-2138
1200 South Hayes Street, Arlington, VA 22202-5050
201 North Craig Street, Suite 102, Pittsburgh, PA 15213-1516
RAND URL: http://www.rand.org/
To order RAND documents or to obtain additional information, contact Distribution Services: Telephone: (310) 451-7002; Fax: (310) 451-6915; Email: order@rand.org

Preface

This research project began by asking the question "Is there a role for scientists in K–12 educational reform efforts?"[1] Judging by the investment that federal funding agencies have made toward programs designed to utilize the expertise of scientists in K–12 reform, it would seem that many feel that there is indeed a role for those trained in science in K–12 education. Highly competent, skilled scientists are a rich resource in our society that may be useful in strengthening science and mathematics education in schools across the country. It seems, appropriate, therefore to continue to develop effective ways of merging scientists, as resources, into our educational system.

The National Science Foundation (NSF) has funded several initiatives designed to create partnerships between scientists and K–12 classrooms. These partnerships involve scientists at various stages of their careers, ranging from senior, retired scientist to scientists in training. Because of NSF's interest in developing programs specifically designed to partner science graduate students with K–12 classrooms, NSF asked RAND's Science and Technology Policy Institute to study the range of current programs that connect science graduate and undergraduate students to K–12 classrooms.

This report presents the results of that study. The goal of this research was to identify the impacts, challenges, and strategies of programs that link science graduate and undergraduate students to K–12 classrooms. Information for this study was gathered from interviews during site visits to eight outreach programs. Many of the challenges these programs faced were not limited to the K–12 classrooms but were related to the broader issue of creating university-school partnerships as a strategy for science education reform.

This report should interest those in university communities involved in implementing or participating in outreach programs. It should also be of interest to federal policymakers who are concerned with science education reform and the development of partnerships between universities and K–12 schools as a method of improving science learning in classrooms across the country.

---

[1]In this instance, we use the word *scientist* to broadly refer both to those trained in scientific disciplines and to those who are in training for scientific careers.

The S&T Policy Institute

Originally created by Congress in 1991 as the Critical Technologies Institute and renamed in 1998, the Science and Technology Policy Institute is a federally funded research and development center sponsored by the National Science Foundation and managed by RAND. The Institute's mission is to help improve public policy by conducting objective, independent research and analysis on policy issues that involve science and technology. To this end, the Institute

- Supports the Office of Science and Technology Policy and other Executive Branch agencies, offices, and councils
- Helps science and technology decisionmakers understand the likely consequences of their decisions and choose among alternative policies
- Helps improve understanding in both the public and private sectors of the ways in which science and technology can better serve national objectives.

Science and Technology Policy Institute research focuses on problems of science and technology policy that involve multiple agencies. In carrying out its mission, the Institute consults broadly with representatives from private industry, institutions of higher education, and other nonprofit institutions.

Inquiries regarding the Science and Technology Policy Institute may be directed to the addresses below.

Helga Rippen
Director
Science and Technology Policy Institute

Science and Technology Policy Institute
RAND
1200 S. Hayes St.
Arlington, VA 22202-5050

Phone: (703) 413-1100, x5574
Web:
http://www.rand.org/scitech/stpi/
Email: stpi@rand.org

Contents

vi

Figures

Tables

Summary

Background

Not since the Sputnik "crisis" has so much public attention focused on improving science education. In the 1950s, concerns were driven by national security fears and focused on increasing the numbers of scientists able to keep the United States ahead of the Soviets during the "space race." The current reform impulse springs from the awareness that U.S. society has become increasingly based on science and technology and requires a science-literate workforce that is able to understand and derive benefits from recent scientific advances. In contrast to the earlier movement, which focused on increasing the number of scientists, this movement emphasizes science for all and promotes changes in science education that will ensure that all students have equal access and opportunities to learn.

To promote education reforms, a number of initiatives have been developed to encourage changes in teaching practices that will ultimately improve student learning in science. Some of these initiatives include *Science for All Americans* (American Association for the Advancement of Science), Project 2061's *Benchmarks for Science Literacy* (American Association for the Advancement of Science), and the *National Science Education Standards* (NSES). The NSES, released by the National Research Council in 1996, is one of the more prominent sets of guidelines among these initiatives. Known simply as the Standards, the National Science Education Standards encourage an inquiry-based approach to teaching science that enables students to explore learning on their own and encourages teachers to facilitate this process rather than control it.

For some K–12 classrooms, this new method of teaching science has created challenges. One consequence of many of the Standards' recommendations is a need for increased classroom time for science instruction because the use of kits and other supplemental material requires additional setup and cleanup time. Moreover, current reforms emphasize covering fewer topics in greater depth than a traditional textbook-based curriculum and require teachers to address students' scientific thinking more directly. Finally, teachers are challenged to develop sophisticated classroom managerial skills to get multiple (perhaps as many as eight) groups of students to remain simultaneously "on task" with their science lesson.

As a consequence of these challenges, mechanisms to support K–12 classrooms in their efforts to implement these new teaching practices are different and more demanding than those needed to support more-traditional practices in the classroom. In many instances, these reforms create extra requirements, such as content experts and curriculum specialists to ensure that, through inquiry-based learning, students are guided to a deeper and richer understanding of science. Often, another set of hands is necessary to help with all the different group activities that are going on in the classrooms.

To support the recent changes in K–12 instruction, many schools are involved in outreach programs that partner them with local universities. Partnerships with universities can support teaching instruction in a number of ways. Universities can provide instructional materials and resources to teachers to aid in science instruction; facilities, such as laboratories, to give students and teachers opportunities to experience hands-on science; and human capital in the form of university scientists who can work with teachers and K–12 students in a variety of ways. Science graduate and undergraduate students are another important university resource, and many outreach programs have found ways to utilize the talents and skills of these students. These science students may prove to be an invaluable resource in supporting K–12 classrooms in improving science education. Indicative of this trend, the NSF has expanded efforts to use science graduate students in outreach programs by creating the Graduate Teaching Fellows in K–12 (GK–12) program. This program provides fellowships for science graduate students (and some advanced undergraduates) to serve as resources to support teachers in science and math instruction in K–12 classrooms. Very little is known about these outreach programs and the effects they have on K–12 classrooms or on the science students that participate in the programs. As these programs proliferate, understanding their impacts and identifying the features of successful programs are crucial for informing the policy decisions about how best to help K–12 classrooms improve science learning.

This research study examines the utilization of science graduate and undergraduate students in K–12 educational reform efforts and specifically addresses three main questions:

1. What are the impacts and challenges of outreach programs for different participants in K–12 schools?

2. What are the impacts and challenges of outreach programs for different participants in institutions of higher education?

3. What are some of the features of programs that effectively address these challenges?

Using a case-study methodology, the RAND research team obtained information for this study from site visits to eight outreach programs across the country.[2] Although all the programs had similar goals—enhancing K–12 science education through partnerships with universities—the approaches differed. The majority of the programs we visited were direct classroom enhancement programs in which science graduate and undergraduate students worked in the classroom with teachers to support learning. However, we also visited programs that placed teachers in the laboratories with graduate students, programs in which science graduate and undergraduate students developed and maintained instructional materials for K–12 classrooms, and programs that utilized the science content knowledge of graduate and undergraduate students via the Internet.

This report presents the findings from our research study. Based on interviews with K–12 teachers, university students, program administrators, and university faculty involved with these programs, this report presents their views on the major impacts and challenges of these programs. This report also attempts to synthesize much of the information that was gathered and identify issues for future research on these programs.

Impacts of Outreach Programs

On K–12 Teachers and Students

Most of the outreach programs we selected for site visits focused their outreach activities on schools in underserved, urban communities. Schools in these communities often required more resources to implement many of the recommendations for science education reform. As many studies have shown, urban schools typically have fewer teachers with backgrounds in science or math; classrooms are often overcrowded; and the teachers in these schools often face classrooms of students having a wide range of learning abilities. Under these conditions, teaching science can be difficult not only because of the subject-matter expertise but also because of the larger societal conditions that prevail in these schools. Thus, it was not surprising that many of these programs had impacts not only on the improvement of the science content knowledge of teachers and students but also on the "spirit" of teaching science. Interviews with K–12 teachers revealed that some of the most significant effects of the programs were the attitudinal changes, as well as the changes in teaching practices. Teachers reported spending more time teaching science, being more comfortable

---

[2]To ensure confidentiality of the interviewees, the names of the outreach programs and the affiliated universities are not included in this report.

teaching science, and feeling better serving as facilitators, rather than dictators, of science learning. Moreover, many of the K–12 teachers reported an increased sense of collegiality toward other science teachers, which contributed to a sense of professionalism. Teachers stated that participating in an outreach program together created a common bond that provided the basis for more dialogue, interaction, and discussion of different methods of teaching science. We did not interview K–12 students, but teachers reported that their students displayed greater enthusiasm toward science and that students who had often been disinterested or difficult to engage were now active participants in classroom activities. For programs that brought science students into the classrooms to work with the teachers, many teachers reported that the relationship between the K–12 students and the university students was a key ingredient for motivating and engaging the students in their science lessons.

Interviews with participants across the different programs indicated that the primary contribution of the science students was their ability to expedite many of the reforms that were currently taking place. Most of the programs were infusing schools with resources toward the goal of enhancing science learning. However, the university science students acted as true catalysts by creating optimal conditions for these changes to occur and thereby speeding up a process that might still have occurred eventually but perhaps have taken longer. Time is a serious issue, particularly for students in urban schools. For each year of incremental progress toward changing teacher attitude and gradually changing teacher practices, a generation of students may be losing opportunities to develop the solid foundation in math and science necessary to contribute to a society increasingly steeped in science and technology. Thus, even as the outreach programs were taking steps toward building better practices in science, the university science students could expedite this process by providing the science content expertise and the support teachers needed to achieve more-immediate changes in the classroom.

On University Science Students and Community Relations

The outreach programs also had a number of impacts on the universities that sponsored them. Science graduate and undergraduate students reported that participation in these programs provided them with a more in-depth learning and understanding of science. Although many of the graduate students had worked as teaching assistants, many found that having to teach and explain scientific concepts to a broader audience forced them to think more deeply about their own understanding of science. Furthermore, many science students felt their communication skills had also improved as a result of interacting with K–12 teachers and students. Students working with teachers in K–12 classrooms reported that the experience of doing outreach in urban schools made them much more aware of the importance of educational resources and their impact on learning. These students were acutely aware of the difficulties teachers face: classrooms in which the motivation to learn is low and classroom management takes precedence over learning, as well as the challenge of teaching science to students who have difficulty reading at grade level.

We noted that these programs were attractive to science students for a variety of reasons, but primarily because of the opportunity to use their scientific knowledge to help others. Despite the fact that most of the programs offered monetary compensation, few of the graduate students participated in these programs solely for the money. The graduate students we spoke with wanted a broader experience and felt that their participation in outreach to K–12 students and teachers was more valuable than their work as teaching assistants. Undergraduate students, however, did report that the monetary compensation influenced their decisions to participate in outreach programs. Moreover, most felt that participation in outreach programs would prove beneficial to their career objectives.

The outreach programs also appeared to have broader institutional impacts. Discussions with university program directors, coordinators, and managers indicated that better credibility and improved relations with the local community were some of the benefits for the university.[3] Engaging in activities to improve the local schools enhanced the image of the institution in the eyes of the community. Moreover, many program directors reported that K–12 teachers took pride in their affiliation and connection with the institution and that this went a long way toward community building.

A few of the university program directors suggested that these outreach programs could also make science courses more attractive to students. As one program manager explained, engaging undergraduate science majors in outreach programs is good for the university. Undergraduate science core requirements typically have low approval ratings among many of the science and nonscience majors. Thus, linking science courses to outreach programs, a feature that most university students rate highly, may be one way to engage students and also solve strategic community problems.

---

[3]In this context, *program director* refers to the university faculty member who is in charge of the outreach program, not to the program director within the federal agency that is sponsoring the outreach program. Program coordinators and managers are the staff members responsible for coordinating the efforts of the program. Typically, these persons are more involved in the day-to-day detailed work than is the program director.

Because these outreach programs offered a unique type of teaching and learning experience for graduate students, some program directors felt that these programs could be instrumental in reshaping and improving graduate education. Furthermore, some program directors believed that participating in outreach could benefit graduate students by helping them with their teaching skills, which was perceived as an added benefit to the university, particularly since many graduate students later serve as teaching assistants for undergraduate science courses.

Challenges of Outreach Programs

Outreach programs that bridge the gap between universities and K–12 schools face unique challenges from each of these cultures. As we spoke with the different program participants, a clear pattern emerged in the description and identification of the challenges. In the minds of many of the interviewees that worked primarily in the K–12 schools—such as teachers, program coordinators and managers—the major challenges associated with outreach had to do with the implementation of the programs, that is, the obstacles and barriers they faced in trying to put the outreach programs into practice. Program directors, who mostly worked with the university, described the challenges to sustainability, discussing the obstacles and barriers associated with creating and sustaining these programs as integral components of the university.

Implementation

The curricular priorities of the district created the major implementation challenges for some of the outreach programs. The need to improve student achievement in math and literacy skills in urban or low-income rural school districts often takes precedence over the need to improve science instruction. Consequently, the time available for science instruction is limited. Program coordinators and managers reported that outreach programs were put on hold frequently during test time so that classrooms could focus on "skill and drill exercises" in preparation for upcoming district and state tests. Moreover, the emphasis on classroom discipline in many inner-city school districts created potential conflicts with the "hands-on" nature of the classroom-based outreach programs.

Sustainability

The main challenges from the university side were based on the culture of universities. All of the universities we visited were classified as Research I universities and thus emphasize research as the most valued aspect of university work, leading to what many felt was an extremely narrow focus for graduate education. Many felt that the culture of the university, and particularly the science departments, fostered an environment that devalued teaching and discouraged any activities that might distract graduate students from their focus on research.

Another challenge was a lack of moral support for outreach programs among science faculty. The reasons ranged from benign disinterest to active opposition to the fundamental concept of the outreach program itself. For example, one interviewee stated "Most faculty don't want to be bothered with educational outreach because it hinders research productivity." Other faculty were skeptical of education outreach programs and viewed them as having very little impact on achieving the stated goals.

A final challenge involved turf issues between education and science faculty. Many program directors acknowledge that there are often territorial issues between schools of education and the physical sciences that created challenges when faculty from these two groups tried to work together. The primary challenge between these two groups centered on the emphasis on content knowledge versus pedagogical training. Despite these challenges, collaboration with schools of education was critical to the success of many of these programs. In addition to providing pedagogical training for the graduate and undergraduate science students, some programs used student-teacher interns to accompany science students into classrooms as part of their training. In many instances, visible support and involvement from schools of education gave outreach programs more credibility in the eyes of the K–12 community.

Characteristics of Effective Programs

Among the outreach programs we visited, we identified a set of shared characteristics that enabled these outreach programs to deal effectively with many of the challenges outlined above. These characteristics are discussed below and may have important implications for designing effective outreach programs.

Shared Vision

Outreach programs require an extraordinary amount of support and dedication from program participants. Conversations with program directors, coordinators, and managers indicated that a critical part of gaining this dedication is a shared vision of the importance of the outreach program. The vision is a unifying force that serves to inspire and bring together program participants from diverse backgrounds. Program participants shared a vision that not only encompassed larger societal aims, such as social justice, addressing problems of inequity, and preparing leaders for tomorrow's society, but also the belief that these objectives could be met through improved science learning. Thus, improving student learning in science was considered a means to an end, but not the end itself.

Personnel

Many interviewees stated that programs and efforts like this could not be replicated without the involvement of certain kinds of key individuals. In fact, the term "magicians" was used to describe these all-important individuals who were able to make things happen seemingly out of thin air. Each program had a magician and we were able to identify similar characteristics among these individuals that made them stand out. Typically, these individuals were

- senior faculty
- familiar with the intricacies of the university system and understood how it worked
- viewed as eminent in their discipline
- not concerned with maintaining the status quo.

This list is not meant to imply that individuals without these characteristics cannot contribute to a successful program, but the consistency of these four characteristics across all of the outreach programs we researched underscores their importance.

Strategic Planning

Perhaps the most critical aspect in the success of many of these programs was having the time and available funding necessary for strategic planning. Although most programs were initially supported on limited budgets, there was plenty of freedom and flexibility for strategic planning. Most program directors felt that, by starting off small, they had the ability to construct the programs the way they wanted to without having to deal with "the strings that are often attached" to federal or private funding. This also meant they had the time to select the appropriate personnel and build a solid base of trust between the university and the schools.

Infrastructure Support

It is not uncommon for outreach programs outside of science and math to utilize graduate and undergraduate students. For example, social science and humanities departments often have outreach programs with similar goals that utilize the skills and talents of undergraduate and graduate students. Finding ways to link to ongoing programs and similar efforts is important in building an infrastructure of support for outreach programs within the university. For example, many sociology, psychology, and ethnic studies departments have also participated in different forms of outreach and can offer comments and suggestions about making inroads into district communities. Schools of education can be the most critical support resource for outreach programs; developing partnerships with these schools is one method of connecting the science content with the pedagogical training.

Locality

Proximity is also valuable. Being near one another, particularly when the university is an integral part of the same community, allowed the university and K–12 schools to develop much stronger bonds than otherwise. Moreover, science students who could walk to the K–12 schools were able to spend more of time in the classroom with students than in traveling to and from the schools.

Implications and Issues for Further Study

This research was designed to shine a spotlight on a few programs and raise issues for further exploration. Thus, any follow-up work should be aimed at verifying the impacts and challenges identified in this study. However, we believe that one of the important implications here is an awareness of the different ways that outreach programs can impact student learning. Although a single outreach program cannot be expected to provide all the resources needed to improve science and math learning in K–12 classrooms, good outreach programs can support classrooms and provide the necessary infrastructure to ensure that student learning in science and math is not compromised while schools are in the process of change. As schools begin developing more rigorous science and math curricula, attracting and retaining teachers with strong backgrounds in math and science, and creating instructional activities aimed at engaging students of all backgrounds, science graduate and undergraduate students can serve as an important tool for aiding and expediting that process. However, for programs to capitalize on the diverse talent pool of these students, we offer the issues in the following subsections for further research:

Evaluation Issues

Understanding the Benefits of the University Science Students. The classroom-centered programs all raise the question of whether their main benefits flow from the enhanced science expertise the science students provide or merely from having of an extra set of hands.

Measuring Program Impacts. The findings of this study provide a starting point for considering and developing metrics that could be used to evaluate the impacts of these programs. The broad array of impacts suggests the need for multiple metrics to assess programs fully. Moreover, the usual metrics for evaluation, such as an increase in math or science test scores, may not be the most significant or the most appropriate outcomes to expect from these programs. Interviewee comments suggest that some of the greatest impacts were the changes in the attitudes of teachers and students toward science. One may well argue that these sorts of changes are needed before teaching practices can change meaningfully. Assessments geared toward measuring the changes in attitudes toward science may be one way to evaluate the impacts of these programs. Other assessments could focus on skills that combine scientific process knowledge with scientific content knowledge. Teachers clearly felt that their students had a much richer understanding of science than district and state exams indicated and felt that the multiple-choice format of the exams limited the ability of their students to demonstrate their understanding of science. Many suggested that evaluations that assess the ability of their students to set up experiments and carry out different science-related tasks would be better indicators of science learning.

Program impacts should also consider the effects of outreach programs on university science students. Improved communication in science, increased enrollment in science courses as a result of the addition of an outreach component to traditional science classes, and a deeper awareness and understanding of societal issues are all important impacts that were mentioned in this study, and future research should focus on how to measure these impacts. Strong evaluations that measure impacts on both the K–12 classroom and university science students could move these outreach activities from peripheral programs to integral components of the university because they would be viewed as having measurable positive impacts on the graduate students that participate in them, as well as on the K–12 students and teachers.

Finally, evaluation should be ongoing and continuous, built in to each program from the start.

Design Issues

Designing Outreach Programs that Meet the Needs of K–12 Schools. Targeting the needs of the K–12 schools in the most appropriate and effective manner is an important issue in program design. The programs in this report represent a wide range of outreach activities, from those that require little classroom contact (e.g., remote classroom enhancement programs) to the those that involve more sustained classroom interaction (e.g., direct classroom enhancement). Thus, one strategy for targeting a school's needs effectively would be to develop a university-based program that contains a portfolio of different intervention approaches for partnering the talents and skills of university students with K–12 classrooms. This would allow outreach programs more flexibility in coordinating their efforts with K–12 schools. For example, rather than starting out with direct enhancement programs, K–12 schools and universities might elect to begin working together through remote enhancement programs in which graduate students interact via the Internet. If more support is needed over time, the trust and camaraderie that has been built from a nonintrusive method of support can be used to "smooth the way" in developing more intensive methods of outreach.

Creating Pathways to Bring Science and Math Students into Teaching Professions. An important part of improving student learning in science is attracting more teachers with backgrounds in science and math to K–12 classrooms. Subject matter knowledge is important in teaching because it affects the confidence that teachers bring to the subjects they teach and their ability to be creative in developing curriculum. These programs may serve as important filters to identify students with strong science content knowledge and an interest in teaching and working with K–12 schools. Thus, linking students in these programs with other opportunities for teaching may offer one way to channel students into teaching careers.

Implementation Issues

Allowing Time to Build Trust Between Universities and Schools. Many of the implementation issues center on the relationship between the universities and the schools. These relationships must be built on mutual trust and respect between the university and the schools. Because the process of developing relationships built on mutual trust takes time, programs should have more "lead time" for universities and schools to interact with each other. Most program directors commented on the "need to hit the ground running" once funding was secured, and how this haste created an atmosphere of poor decisionmaking and miscommunication.

Supporting and Expanding Existing Programs. Rather than creating new programs from whole cloth, it is likely to be more cost-effective to identify existing programs that have demonstrated some measure of success and expand these programs to other schools and universities. In looking at partnerships, we believe that the characteristics of the university culture are critical to success and that focusing on state-supported colleges and universities or historically minority universities with long histories of community outreach may be one strategy toward overcoming many of the challenges faced with Research I universities.

Acknowledgments

This research is based on interviews with a number of individuals at universities and K–12 schools throughout the United States. The author is therefore indebted to the program directors and coordinators, the university faculty, K–12 teachers, and the graduate and undergraduate students who agreed to be interviewed. Although the interviewees have been promised confidentiality and cannot be acknowledged by name, the author thanks them for their willingness to participate in this study, their candor, and their organizational efforts involved in coordinating the site visits and scheduling interviews.

The author owes a large debt of thanks to several individuals at NSF. Special thanks go to Luther S. Williams for conversations and insights that led to the development and the sponsorship of this project, to John B. Hunt for his guidance throughout the process and for maintaining a sense of humor along the way, and to Joe McInerney for his encouragement and helpful comments on an earlier version of this manuscript.

Several RAND colleagues assisted at various points of the study. The author would like to acknowledge Sheila Kirby and Charles A. Goldman, whose wise counsel in the early stages of the project helped to frame the parameters of this study; Mike Timpane, for his informal review of this report; Jennifer Kawata and Eric Derghazarian, for their research assistance; and David Adamson for tirelessly reading numerous drafts of the report and providing insightful comments and suggestions that helped to shape the analysis of the data.

Finally, the author would like to thank RAND colleague Laura Hamilton and Senta Raizen, Director of National Center for Improving Science Education, who reviewed the manuscript thoroughly and offered comments that greatly enhanced the quality of this report.

Despite the contribution of so many, the author is solely responsible for any errors in the report.

1. Introduction

Not since the Sputnik "crisis" of the 1950s has so much attention focused on improving science education in the United States. Since the mid-1990s, hundreds of new programs to reform science education in various ways have either been created or formalized from prior informal activities.[1]

However, the current wave of science education reform differs from the earlier one in fundamental ways. The reaction to Sputnik was driven primarily by national security concerns growing out of the Cold War with the Soviet Union. Underlying the crisis was a fear that a loss of U.S. scientific preeminence put the nation's security at risk. Accompanying this was the blow to national pride that "losing" the space race represented. Pressure for change arose largely from the scientific establishment, augmented by public outcry, media attention, and heated debate at all levels of government. Response to the crisis focused on how to produce more scientific specialists and restore U.S. ascendance in key scientific fields in the eyes of the world and the American public. Thus, the reforms that emerged from the Sputnik era were most concerned with providing advanced training to the most promising students to create a cadre of premier scientists.

By contrast, the current reform is more concerned with providing science literacy for all citizens and increasing opportunities for traditionally underserved students to have access to advanced scientific knowledge and career opportunities. The crux of the problem in the late 1990s and early 2000s is not the need for more scientific specialists but rather for a more scientifically literate workforce and citizenry. The focus in this current reform centers on economic competitiveness and opportunity rather than national security. Thus, it is not surprising that some of the recent calls for improvement in science education come from the corporate world, especially the high-tech sectors. As one corporate executive stated, "Education in this country is critical. If we don't continue to produce people who drive the process of innovation and technology, we will not succeed."[2] Added pressures for change have also come from government and some quarters of the scientific community. Thus, current attempts to improve science education are not focused on increasing the pool of

---

[1]For a more detailed discussion of the origins of the science education reforms of both the 1960s and the 1980–1990s, see Raizen (1997).

[2]Quoted in Popper, Wagner, and Larson (1998), p. 101.

Ph.D. scientists but rather on raising the standards for a baseline science education.

The emergence of science and technology as the major engine of U.S. economic development (see Figure 1.1) has created two sets of challenges that make efforts to improve science education paramount. The first challenge is how to sustain this engine—how do we ensure that future generations of workers will have the skills and preparation needed to sustain the scientific and technological needs of the future? As illustrated in Figure 1.1, the advancement of science and technology is fueled by human capital—workers who create, innovate, and develop tomorrow's new technologies. Who will make up this workforce? By 2015, nonwhite Americans will constitute 35 percent of the population and an even greater proportion of the youngest workers, ages 16–25.[3] This trend is projected to continue until the United States will eventually have a "minority majority"—that is, a greater than 50 percent nonwhite population. This is already true in California, the most populous state. Are all groups, including those that are typically underrepresented in science and math, being prepared to contribute to the workforce? Judging from current statistics, the answer seems to be quite clearly no. Student achievement results on tests administered by the National Assessment of Educational Progress (NAEP) indicate that for the most part, students are performing at higher levels in mathematics and science than did their counterparts in the late 1970s; however, a greater number of black and Hispanic students perform at basic proficiency levels than their white and Asian counterparts (NCES, 1997).

RAND*MR1446-1.1*

Science and technology

- Societal issues
  - Scientifically literate society
  - Fair distribution of economic opportunities

- Human capital issues
  - Quality of workforce
  - Diversity of workforce

Science education

Figure 1.1—Relationship Between Scientific and Technological
Advancement and Science Education

_____

[3]Projections developed from data from the 2000 U.S. Census.

The second challenge relates to the equity issues created by a society increasingly reliant on science and technology. Who will reap the rewards of innovations in science and technology? Who will bear the risks? Scientific developments in health care, agriculture, and information technology have created the need for a scientifically literate society able to understand the long-term consequences of these recent advances. Moreover, economic opportunities for jobs and resources will favor those who have a sound and thorough understanding of science. Consequently, science education that prepares all students to contribute to and to benefit from opportunities made available in this society is absolutely crucial.

Standards-Based Reforms Create New Classroom Needs

In response to growing concerns about the state of science education, several initiatives were developed to guide the current reform movement. In the 1980s, the American Chemical Society (ACS), the Biological Sciences Curriculum Study, the Educational Development Center, the Lawrence Hall of Science, the National Science Resources Center, and the Technical Education Resources Center all developed innovative science curricula. In 1989, the American Association for the Advancement of Science (AAAS), through its Project 2061, published *Science for All Americans,* and in 1993, published *Benchmarks for Science Literacy.*

The most prominent among these guidelines are the National Science Education Standards, which undergird the current standards-based science reform. Released in 1996 by the National Research Council, the Standards (as they are commonly called) are designed to guide our nation toward a scientifically literate society. A hallmark of the Standards is their emphasis on inquiry-based approaches to science learning. *Inquiry-based approaches* refers to a set of teaching practices that encourage students to formulate questions and devise ways to answer them. Students collect data and decide how to represent them, organize data to generate knowledge, and test the reliability of the knowledge they have generated. As they proceed, students explain and justify their work to themselves and to one another, learn to cope with such problems as the limitations of equipment, and react to challenges that the teacher and classmates pose. At all stages of inquiry, teachers guide, focus, challenge, and encourage student learning.[4] An important component of inquiry-based approaches to science learning is its reliance on prepackaged sets of science materials and workbooks to be used in science lessons (often referred to as *kits*) rather than

---

[4]This definition is paraphrased from National Research Council (1996).

textbooks, and so the Standards also stress the need to create resource-rich classrooms using a multitude of science materials to ensure that students have ample opportunity for engagement during the learning process.

Most of the teachers we interviewed for this study supported the new emphasis on inquiry-based teaching practices. One of the primary reasons was that these practices offered teachers a multidimensional approach to teaching science that allowed them to engage all students regardless of ability level. Many of the teachers we interviewed for this report shared numerous accounts about the difference in their classrooms and their ability to facilitate learning with inquiry-based teaching practices.

At the same time, however, Standards-based reform has created a number of logistical challenges for many classrooms. As a consequence of many of the recommendations from the Standards, more classroom time is required for science instruction because the use of kits and other supplemental material requires additional setup and cleanup time. Moreover, current reforms emphasize covering fewer topics in greater depth than a traditional textbook-based curriculum and require teachers to address students' scientific thinking more directly. Thus, classroom teachers are encouraged to be, as one interviewee noted, "guides on the side" rather than the "sage on the stage." And finally, teachers are challenged to develop sophisticated classroom managerial skills to get multiple (perhaps as many as eight) groups of students to remain simultaneously "on task" with their science lesson.

As a consequence of these challenges, mechanisms to support the efforts of K–12 classrooms to implement standards are different and more demanding than those needed to support more traditional practices in the classroom. Teachers often need to enlist the aid of content experts and resource specialists to ensure that the inquiry-based learning guides students to a deeper and richer understanding of science. Moreover, teachers also need another set of hands to help with all the different group activities that are going on in the classrooms.

The Need for Outreach Programs

Education outreach programs, particularly those that link universities and K–12 schools, are potentially attractive mechanisms for acquiring the type of support necessary to adapt to standards-based reform in K–12 classrooms. Our research identified more than 200 education outreach programs that linked K–12 schools to universities. Typically, federal agencies, private foundations, or corporations support these outreach efforts. Within academic scientific disciplines, outreach activities to K–12 schools are often funded as part of larger university research grants that stipulate that part of the funding be used for educational purposes. This gives universities considerable freedom in deciding on the type of outreach activity to develop and implement.

Typically, these outreach activities are based on one or more of the following strategies to improve science learning in K–12 classrooms:

- **Enhanced professional development for science teachers.** Many teachers of science and math are currently teaching outside their fields. About 56 percent of high school students taking physical science are taught by out-of-field teachers, as are 27 percent of those taking mathematics. These percentages are much greater in high-poverty areas. Among schools with the highest minority enrollments, students have less than a 50-percent chance of getting a science or mathematics teacher who holds both a license and a degree in the field being taught (NCMS, 2000). Thus, one set of strategies focuses on professional development programs that offer opportunities for teachers to broaden and deepen their disciplinary and pedagogical knowledge of science and math.

- **Improved curriculum design.** Curriculum design programs are based on the notion that U.S. science curricula are too diffuse and superficial: "a mile wide and an inch deep." Curriculum design strategies seek to focus and enhance science curricula through classroom experiments and hands-on kits rather than just the use of textbooks.

- **Reforming science pedagogy.** Closely coupled to strategies for curriculum design are strategies for changing the pedagogy of teaching science. Studies in the early 1980s of hands-on science and the lecture-and-textbook approach found the comparisons to favor the hands-on programs (Bredderman, 1983; Shymanky, 1989). Thus, many pedagogical changes focus on having students uncover learning at their own pace, using inquiry-based approaches that are centered on the student rather than on the teacher (Anderson, 1999).

- **Boosting student motivation.** Finally, strategies that seek to motivate and inspire students are based on the idea that students are uninspired by science or that students that begin with interest in science are quickly turned off by the dry lecture "factoid" approach.

Despite the limited number of strategies we examined, our research indicated that there is great variety in the type of activities that universities have developed for outreach. These activities vary in four important ways: the structure of the program, the type of outreach, the kind of K–12 school partnered with, and the student population involved.

The structure of these partnerships can vary tremendously. Some partnerships link specific academic departments (e.g., biology, chemistry or physics) and a neighboring school; other partnerships are formed within education departments that link to K–12 schools but utilize science faculty from a particular department for the outreach activities; still others primarily rely on efforts of an individual faculty member to establish and maintain contacts with K–12 schools. Types of programs include after-school activities, classroom demonstrations, lectures about careers in science, and "be a scientist for a day" programs. These programs also vary in the type of K–12 school they work with, ranging from schools that have limited resources for science instruction to affluent private schools interested in cutting-edge technology. The student populations vary as well, from students who have expressed minimal interest and aptitude in science to college-bound, high-achieving students likely to choose careers in science and research.

Partnerships with universities also offer a number of resources to K–12 schools for improving science and math education. Universities have the facilities; the technology; and perhaps most importantly, the human resources to support K–12 classrooms in their efforts to improve science learning. Our research indicated that science education outreach programs involve all levels of "scientific experts" in their activities and that programs that specifically recruit graduate and undergraduate science majors for outreach activities are somewhat rare. While undergraduates typically participate in outreach programs via student service learning programs, the participation of graduate students in outreach programs is usually more informal. Science graduate students may choose to volunteer their time as needed or work with research advisors who may be involved in outreach programs. However, recently the utilization of science students in education outreach programs has recently become more formalized. For example, teacher-scientist programs that typically relied on science faculty to work with teachers in the laboratory have developed ways to encourage graduate students to become involved. Partnerships with graduate students are often a better match than those with science professors, who are often busy with their own research activities and may be far removed from the K–12 world. These programs have filled a unique niche in outreach efforts because they allow graduate students to remain linked to their research and yet relate their science to a broader audience.

Rationale for the Study

Placing graduate and undergraduate students in the classrooms to support teachers in K–12 science and math instruction is another way programs are using the scientific expertise of university science students in science education reform efforts. In 1998, the National Science Foundation (NSF) created the Graduate Teaching Fellows in K–12 Education (GK–12) program. The GK–12 program provides fellowships for science graduate students (and some advanced undergraduates) to serve as resources for teachers in science and math instruction in K–12 classrooms. GK–12 fellows receive $18,000 per year to spend 10 to 15 hours a week aiding teachers in classroom instruction. This program came under intense scrutiny in mid-2000, when the NSF director requested an increase in the FY2001 budget for this program. Questions have been raised in Congress about the prudence of using graduate students in K–12 classrooms and about expanding a program before any evaluation has been carried out.

The need for evaluation raises the broader question of what is known about programs that, like GK–12, seek to utilize the scientific expertise of graduate and undergraduate students in K–12 education reform. As these programs proliferate, understanding their impacts and identifying the features that distinguish successful programs from not-so-successful ones is crucial in informing the policy decisions about how best to help K–12 classrooms improve science learning. Highly competent and skilled science graduate students are a valuable human resource in our society that may be useful in strengthening science instruction in schools across the country. It is important that we develop the most effective ways of using these graduate students in our educational system.

The Research Questions

This research study examined outreach programs that utilize the scientific expertise of graduate and undergraduate students in K–12 education and addressed three main questions:

1. What are the impacts and challenges of outreach programs for different participants within K–12 schools?

2. What are the impacts and challenges of outreach programs for different participants within the institutions of higher education they partner with?

3. What are some features of programs that addressed these challenges effectively ?

Clearly, the educational bottom line for these programs is their impact on student achievement. This research study, however, takes a step back and first identifies the impacts the programs have on different participants. What are these programs doing? Who is being affected and how? Are these impacts linked to student achievement? Moreover, this study examines the impacts on *all* participants in outreach programs, not just on K–12 classrooms. The second research question is based on an understanding that, for programs to have meaningful impacts, there must first be some sustainability. An often neglected question concerning programs that partner universities and K–12 schools is "What do institutions of higher education gain from partnerships with K–12 schools?" Moreover, what policies can be put in place to strengthen links between universities and K–12 schools that result in long-term sustainable programs? Finally, the third research question seeks to identify a shared set of features among these outreach programs that might inform us on how to design more-effective programs. Information from this research should contribute to the design of metrics of effectiveness for other programs with similar goals and strategies and should identify several of the key issues involved in program design and assessment to guide more-comprehensive efforts at scaling up and evaluating similar programs.

Research Approach and Methodology

To address these questions, the RAND project team conducted an exploratory, case-study effort to examine eight outreach programs that utilize graduate and undergraduate science students. We interviewed several participants in these programs about program impacts, challenges, and strategies for developing effective programs. This report summarizes the interview data that was gathered. The comments are organized by the different themes that emerged from conversations with program participants. Thus, unless otherwise noted, all comments and assertions made within this report are based solely on interviews. When necessary, direct quotations are used to emphasize certain points but are not used to justify or validate a particular viewpoint or perspective. One of the primary aims of this study is to identify the types of research issues that need in-depth exploration so that the effects of these outreach programs can be better understood. Another potential outcome of this study is to explore the usefulness of gathering this type of information prior to formal evaluation as one way to better align the program assessments with both anticipated and, particularly, unanticipated program impacts.

The research approach involved three steps: program selection, data collection, and data analysis.

Program Selection

To select the programs for our study, we first compiled a list of over 200 education outreach programs that involved scientists from all levels (e.g., bachelor's, master's, and doctoral degrees in science) and career backgrounds (e.g., academic scientists, industry scientists, engineers). We used a number of different databases to generate this list. RAND's RaDiUS database, which tracks all federally funded research and development activities, allowed us to identify federal science programs across a variety of agencies, including NASA and the departments of Energy, Defense, Agriculture, and Education. We also used the NSF awards database, which allowed us to focus on NSF-sponsored projects. Finally, we used Web search techniques to identify programs funded by private organizations, such as Howard Hughes Medical Institute, or scientific societies, such as the American Chemical Society (ACS), the American Physical Society (APS), and the Federation of American Societies for Experimental Biology (FASEB).

In collaboration with NSF, we developed a list of criteria for selecting programs for site visits. Resource and budget constraints limited the scope of the project, and we decided to focus on one subset of programs. At the time this project, began, the GK–12 program was just under way, and we narrowed the scope of the project to focus only on programs that used graduate and undergraduate science students in their outreach activities. This limited us to approximately 25 programs that had significant involvement of this group of early career scientists in their outreach activities.

From the 25 programs, we narrowed the selection to those that were in existence for more than five years. One of the key research areas we wanted to address in this study is strategies that lead to effective and sustainable outreach programs, so "years of existence" was used as one measure of sustainability. To get at some ideas about effectiveness, we talked with various NSF program directors that had experience working with outreach programs using scientists. We asked them to share with us ideas about what makes a program effective and to suggest some features we might look for in selecting programs.

By this point, we had identified 15 potential programs for study. Because its mission includes supporting activities designed to increase the participation of women and minorities and others underrepresented in science and technology, NSF suggested that, among these programs, we select programs whose outreach activities focused on schools in underserved communities. These schools are characterized by low-income, primarily African-American and Hispanic, students and schools in urban and rural settings. This is an important point because many of these programs had to face difficult circumstances that may not be indicative of most education outreach programs. Over half of the programs we visited were doing outreach under some very tough conditions but where the need for success is perhaps the greatest. This issue is discussed in greater depth in Section 2.

In all, we selected eight programs for site visits. These programs had similar goals: enhancing science education through partnerships with universities. All of the programs were university-based, which means that the funding went to the university and that the outreach activity typically involved sending the scientists out into the schools. Programs differed in their funding, with some programs being solely supported by federal or private funding, and others being supported by both federal and private funding. Programs varied in the grade level targeted, and there was a mix of elementary, middle, and high school grade levels, as well as scientific disciplines targeted. Some programs were as brief as two weeks in the summer, while others were year-round. The programs we selected were in various geographic regions of the country (the Northeast, the Southeast, and the West Coast). The programs differed in the scope of impact, some were districtwide efforts, others were part of school clusters, and others were much smaller partnerships initiated by schools contacting a particular faculty member at the university to initiate the effort. Section 2 discusses the programs in more detail. The names and institutional affiliations of the programs have been withheld to honor guarantees of confidentiality.

Data Collection

The data on which this study is based were collected from interviews with program directors, program coordinators and managers,[5] K–12 teachers, and graduate and undergraduate students that participated in each of the outreach programs we selected. Because of budgetary and logistical constraints, we did not interview K–12 students. Also, many of the interview questions focused on programmatic and implementation issues, and we felt it was more cost-effective to meet with those who were most familiar with these issues.

In all, we conducted 45 interviews with 83 individuals in 8 different programs. Site visits typically lasted 2–3 days and usually included interviews with the program director and 1–2 program coordinators and managers, focus group interviews with teachers (usually 3–4 teachers per focus group), and focus group

---

[5]Program coordinators and managers are staff members responsible for coordinating the efforts of the program. Typically, these persons are more involved in the day-to-day detailed work than the program director.

interviews with graduate students and/or undergraduate students (2–3 students per focus group). The interviews with program directors and program coordinators were individual semistructured interviews and took place at the university affiliated with the outreach program. The interviews followed a standard protocol (see Appendix A), but the conversation was allowed to move beyond the interview questions to explore other issues. These interviews generally lasted one hour, although many went longer. The interviews with the teachers usually took place at the K–12 school and used a focus group format. Focus group interviews generally lasted 2 hours. When possible, a focus group format was also used to interview graduate students, and these interviews took place at the university. Scheduling conflicts with undergraduates made focus group interviews difficult, so they were often individual semistructured interviews. During the site visits, we also attended workshops and seminars; collected materials and literature related to the programs; and in some cases, attended hands-on training sessions with K–12 teachers. While our visits to K–12 schools did not involve classroom observations, we did walk around the schools and take note of the classrooms and the resources available for science instruction.

To encourage complete candor in the responses, we emphasized to the interviewees that this study was not linked to evaluation or funding and promised the participants complete confidentiality. As a result, the interviews were carried out in an atmosphere of relaxed informality that allowed participants to open up and express their thoughts and opinions candidly.

Our interview protocol used similar questions for all the participants, which allowed us to check different responses against different groups and look for corroboration among the responses.

Data Analysis

Our interviews form the basis of the analyses. After the interview tapes had been transcribed, a second researcher read through the interviews and organized the responses based on the frequency with which certain ideas and themes were mentioned. The data were entered into a spreadsheet and grouped according to the source of the comment (e.g., program director, teacher, program manager) and the main theme of the comment. Time and budgetary constraints limited the number of programs we interviewed, and our sample size is too small to make any assertions about true representation or unbiased sampling. Program participants reviewed our analyses to ensure factual accuracy and to have the opportunity to comment.

Organization of the Report

The following sections of the report provide details about the programs examined and the study's main findings. Section 2 describes, in detail, the features and design of the eight programs we visited. The section is intended to provide the reader with a sense of the diversity of the programs and an understanding of the programmatic goals and objectives of each program. Section 3 addresses the first research question in our study by discussing the major impacts and challenges of the outreach programs for K–12 classrooms. Based on interview data gathered primarily from K–12 teachers, this section discusses the effect these programs had on classroom practices, classroom instruction, and student attitudes toward science. Comments from interviewees form the basis for this discussion and are used to articulate and support various themes in the section; they do not necessarily reflect broad or representative opinions on certain topics. Section 4 addresses the question of impacts and challenges from the perspective of university participants. This section draws on comments from program directors, coordinators and managers, and graduate and undergraduate students to discuss impacts on the university as a whole. In identifying some of the challenges within the higher-education culture, this section raises the question of whether outreach programs can offer more benefits to institutions of higher education, and particularly to the university science students that participate in these programs. Section 5, concludes the report by drawing together the different themes presented in earlier sections and discussing the "lessons learned" from these outreach programs. We address the final research question and list the different characteristics that led to the development of sustainable and effective programs. We conclude the section with implications for policy and recommendations for further research.

2. Program Descriptions

This section describes the eight educational outreach programs we examined for this study. We begin this section by discussing some of the features these programs had in common. We follow with a general description of the programs, categorizing them by their approach to enhancing science education. This general description includes the programmatic goals and objectives of the programs and detailed information about their size and scope. This section provides the background information needed for understanding the discussions of impacts and challenges that follow in Sections 3 and 4.

Overview of the Programs

A number of reports have discussed outreach programs and the role that scientists have played in science education reform.[1] This report adds to that body of literature by focusing on programs that utilize graduate and undergraduate science students and their role in science education reform. This report also adds to the literature by focusing on programs that share two key features: long-term experience or commitment (at least five years) to K–12 science education outreach and a particular interest in working across entire school populations in underserved communities, not just with self-selected or gifted students. These two criteria distinguished the programs we examined from virtually all of the other education outreach programs we identified in our initial program selection phase. Although many of those programs also focused on underserved communities, they were not intended for all students but rather only those that had shown interest in science, demonstrated aptitude in science, or attended schools in which there was an awareness of the importance of science education. By contrast, several of the programs included in this study are broadly targeting their outreach activities toward communities and the different schools within these communities.

Outreach programs that focus on underserved communities are especially important for study for a number of reasons:

---

[1]See for example, National Science Resource Center et al. (1997) and Sandia National Laboratories (undated).

- *The persistent achievement gap in math and science.* A tremendous achievement gap between whites and students of color in math and science still exists. Very few strategies seem able to address the different variables that may account for this. Studying outreach programs that show some measure of success in engaging diverse populations in math and science may be the first step in developing creative and innovative ways of solving this problem.

- *Lack of attention to science instruction in elementary grades.* The focus on demonstrating achievement in reading and math on standardized tests often means that other subjects are given less attention in schools in underserved communities. Although this indicates that math is getting adequate attention in many schools, this may not be the case for science, especially in elementary school grades. Middle school teachers we interviewed underscored the importance of beginning science instruction at the earliest possible grades. Thus studying outreach programs that have found ways to bring the focus on science education to elementary grades may offer valuable strategies for success and achievement in science.

- *Schools in underserved communities represent "high-risk, high-payoff" investments.* Although schools in underserved communities offer a number of challenges, a recent RAND report (Grissmer et al., 2000) indicates that federal investments targeted toward students at the lowest end of the socioeconomic spectrum are often the most effective in yielding performance gains. Thus, it makes sense to study programs for which the value of the outreach may be greatest.

With two exceptions, all the programs selected shared this common feature of being engaged in outreach activities in underserved communities. The other two programs had a particularly successful history of outreach, and we felt this aspect would be useful in our discussion and analysis of successful strategies.

Program Characteristics

The primary goal of all of the programs we visited was the enhancement of K–12 science or math instruction. Most programs tried to align their outreach with the standards-based reform recommendations and supported the emphasis on inquiry-based science instruction. However, the approaches these programs used to enhance science instruction differed. Some programs sought to encourage inquiry-based teaching practices by pairing teachers with graduate students in research laboratories. Other programs supported K–12 classrooms through Web-based technology that allows students to ask scientific questions of graduate students via e-mail. Still other programs placed graduate students in the classroom with teachers to help implement inquiry-based practices in the classroom. In the next subsection, we describe in detail the different approaches used to improve science learning in K–12 classrooms. The following categories group the outreach programs in our study according to method of intervention: direct classroom enhancement, teacher preparation, teacher researcher, remote classroom enhancement, and development of instructional materials. We use these categories throughout this report when referring to comments from program participants. Table 2.1 summarizes some of the characteristics of the eight outreach programs. A more detailed explanation of each program is given in Appendix B.

Description of the Different Program Approaches

Direct Classroom Enhancement Programs

This category describes a set of programs in which science graduate and/or undergraduate students work in classrooms with K–12 teachers to support them in science and math instruction. Our interviews and discussions with teachers and graduate students in these programs indicated that support from graduate and undergraduate students often means assisting teachers in setting up different science experiments and activities, explaining challenging scientific concepts to the students, working with teachers in the classroom to observe and help different groups of students, and assisting with curriculum development. We also found that, in some instances, particularly with the graduate students, the support can mean teaching. Most programs encouraged graduate students and teachers to meet prior to classroom activities to discuss how they should work together in the classrooms, but many teachers and students often said they had difficulty finding time for this. Teachers and graduate students alike commented on an initial period of awkwardness when first working together in the classroom. However, for many, this awkwardness dissolved within a few weeks. Student scheduling concerns typically determined the placement of students in particular classrooms, and this was particularly challenging for undergraduates. If a student had an opening in his or her schedule during a time that science is taught in the classroom, the student was paired with the teacher in that classroom. With graduate students, there was more variation. For example, a graduate student may be more comfortable with middle and high school students and so would be placed in these grades. In some cases, teachers would request a student based on a specific content need, such as physics or chemistry. All the teachers we interviewed wanted to have graduate and undergraduate

Table 2.1

Characteristics of Outreach Programs

Name[a]	Funding Source	Grade Level	Scope of Impact	Duration	School Community	Number of Participating Science Students	Time on Outreach	Compensation
DCE1	NSF	K–12	6 public schools	Academic yr.; Summer	Urban	7 grad. students, 17 undergrads	15–20 hrs/wk	Stipend
DCE2	NSF	K–5	68 elem schs; 1,700 teachers; 35,000 students	Academic yr.	Urban	175 undergrads	3–4 hrs/wk	University credit
DCE3	NIH	Middle sch.	6 middle schs; >300 students	Academic yr.	Urban	43 grad. students	Min. 6 hrs/mo	Stipend
TP1	University	Middle sch. High sch.	>100 math majors placed in urban schools	Academic yr.	Urban	13 undergrads	5 hrs/wk	Stipend; Teaching cert.
TR1	Private found.; Research center support	Middle sch. High sch.	25 teachers/yr; Ongoing support of prior participants	2–5 weeks summer; Yr.-round support	Suburban; Urban Rural	8 grad. students	Depends on research project	TA credit
TR2	NSF	Middle sch. High sch.	6 teachers/summer	1st summ, 6 wks; 2nd summ., 4 wks; Acad. yr. support	Suburban, rural	6 scientists	Depends on research project	None—voluntary
RC1	NSF; University	K–12	11 teachers	Academic yr.	Rural	4 undergrads, 12 grad. students	Varies	None—voluntary
IMD1	NSF; Private found.; University	Middle sch. High sch.	3,500 students	Academic yr.	Rural	6 undergrads	10 hrs/wk	Stipend

NOTE: Information in this table is based on the program descriptions presented in Appendix II.

[a] Program name is an acronym of the program approach – direct classroom enhancement (DCE); teacher preparation (TP); teacher researcher (TR); remote classroom enhancement (RC), and instructional materials development (IMD)

students work with them in their classrooms. Depending on the program, students can spend as little as 3 hours per week in a classroom to up to 20 hours per week. Because of the demands on student time, most of these programs offer some sort of compensation for participation in the outreach program. In the case of undergraduate students, student service learning points or university credit hours toward core requirements were used to compensate students for their time. Graduate students, on the other hand, received a stipend as compensation for their time and effort.

Teacher-Preparation Program

This program was an outgrowth of a direct classroom enhancement program that placed graduate students into K–12 classrooms to support teachers in science and mathematics instruction. Having assessed that the need for well-trained teachers in underserved communities was a critical issue in many of the schools in the surrounding community, the director restructured the outreach program so that funding traditionally used to support one graduate student was now used to support the training of undergraduate science and math majors to become K–12 teachers. Although this program has now evolved into a teacher preservice program, we include it because of the years of experience this program has in placing math graduate students in K–12 classrooms. We believed that the program directors and coordinators would have a rich history to draw on in discussing some of the challenges in implementing "GK–12 like" programs. Moreover, because the program, in the end, found more value in preparing undergraduate science and math majors for teaching careers, we felt that the program participants could raise some important concerns about the ultimate goals and objectives of the GK–12 program and others similar to it. Some of the unique aspects of this program are its uncompromising stance on the importance of preparing math and science majors for teaching careers and its focus on recruiting students of color into the teacher-preparation program. Because recruiting math and science majors into teaching careers can be a challenge, this program focuses on identifying math and science majors as early as their junior year in college. The mathematics component of this program is a joint collaboration between the Mathematics Department and the School of Education and recruits junior and senior undergraduate math majors to K–12 schoolteaching careers. During their senior year, undergraduates have an opportunity to intern in school classrooms. The internship experience, which is offered during the winter and spring quarters, involves approximately five hours of classroom participation per week with an individual stipend. A considerable amount of student tutoring and teaching is involved in the classroom participation. The fifth year consists of a full year's teaching experience under an emergency teaching credential with a parallel seminar on student teaching followed by additional coursework the next summer. Students who complete the program receive a university-recommended single-subject teaching credential with a cross-cultural language and academic development emphasis and a Master of Education degree.

Teacher Researcher Programs

This category refers to a set of programs that paired teachers (usually high school teachers) with graduate students in research laboratories. The graduate students in these programs serve as mentors to teachers engaging in laboratory research. In these typically year-round programs, teachers work with the graduate students during the summer on a research project and use the project as the basis for developing science projects or science activities for students in the fall. Depending on the program, the summer workshop can last either two weeks or six weeks. In addition to research, teachers also have opportunities to share ideas with fellow teachers about ways to incorporate what they have learned into their daily classroom practices and curriculum development. During the academic year, graduate students continue to interact and support the teachers either through classroom visits or via e-mail where graduate students are available to address any questions the teachers may have as they transfer their summer projects to the classroom. In many instances, it may be questions related to using a particular technique, such as gel electrophoresis or thin-layer chromatography. These programs focus on learning new techniques and developing curriculums that can enhance science learning in the classrooms. Many of these programs developed as a result of science education reform that recommended inquiry-based learning serve as the foundation for science instruction. Because many teachers did not have opportunities to experience inquiry-based learning themselves, the purpose of these programs is to give teachers "real life" experience doing science and an understanding of what the process of science is all about. To be selected for these programs, teachers fill out applications describing their science background and interests. Graduate students we interviewed stated that they generally selected teachers based on the scientific interests of the teachers. These programs do not exclusively recruit graduate students as partners for science teachers, and teachers have opportunities to work with researchers in industry, as well as science professors. Depending on the program, graduate students that participate in this program can earn either a stipend or credit hours toward their graduate degrees.

Remote Classroom Enhancement Programs

This program supports K–12 teachers in their science instruction by bringing the scientific expertise of graduate students into the classroom via e-mail. Formulating and articulating questions is an important part of inquiry-based science, and this program helps students to develop this skill by providing a means for them to ask scientific experts different science-related questions. The graduate students primarily serve as content experts in answering these questions. This program exhibits the most variation in how it is used to enhance science learning because teachers decide when and how to use the expertise of the graduate students. In some instances, program use can be highly structured, developing the questions to send to the graduate students as a rigorous classroom exercise, or can be more recreational, as a reward for good classroom behavior. Participation in this program is voluntary for both the graduate students and the K–12 classroom teachers. The program design allows the graduate students to decide the degree to which they want to participate in this program. This program welcomes participation from all levels of scientists, not just graduate students, although graduate students constitute a substantial number of the participants. Many of the scientists we spoke to said that they enjoyed participating in this program because it helped them articulate ideas and broaden their knowledge about many different science topics.

Development of Instructional Materials

This program developed instructional materials that can be incorporated into science curriculums for grades 5–12. Undergraduates, assisted by local high school students, assume the main responsibility for building and maintaining different instructional materials. Undergraduates also support teachers and improve their teaching skills during the academic year by introducing these materials into local science classes. Because undergraduates generally have more time than graduate students, they represent the major workforce in this program. Students are selected mainly for their communication skills, and students are given a stipend for working 30 hours/week.

3. Outreach Programs: The Perspective from K–12 Classrooms

This section addresses the first research question of our study, about the impacts and challenges of outreach programs for different participants within K–12 schools. Since this research is not an evaluation, but exploratory, we also needed to discover what is known about such outreach programs, characterizing what they do and identifying their impacts. The issue for us is thus ultimately not how well the program is meeting the purposes for which it was established but what differences the program has made in the teaching of science in K–12 classrooms, why people did things differently, and (when possible) what specific aspect of the program allowed participants to do something differently.

We begin by describing the K–12 schools and communities that participated in these outreach programs. A discussion of the classroom impacts on both the teacher and the K–12 students follows. Because we did not interview the K–12 classroom students, we relied on the teachers to describe the impacts they observed on their students. Our discussion of impacts leads to the next section, which explores the challenges these programs faced in their efforts to enhance science learning in these schools. We conclude with some thoughts about the implications of the findings reported in this section.

Outreach Programs and K–12 Schools

The majority of the outreach programs we visited partnered with public schools in urban communities and used direct classroom enhancement and teacher-preparation approaches. The remaining outreach programs worked with public schools in rural areas and with private schools in suburban areas. These outreach programs used the teacher-researcher and remote classroom enhancement approaches. It was difficult to estimate the number and types of schools that used the latter approach for outreach. Although originally designed for teachers and students in rural communities, Internet technology makes this program accessible to any classroom.

Schools became involved in the outreach activities by a variety of methods. One of the largest programs we visited was part of a districtwide reform effort, and all the district's schools were involved. Other outreach programs chose to work with a small set of schools in the immediate vicinity of the university and to begin developing relationships with individual teachers in the schools to identify their needs and explore possibilities for outreach. Approaching schools at the teacher level was a common strategy among many of the outreach programs. For many of the programs, relationships with teachers had already been cultivated through graduate schools of education. In fact, most of the universities had established relationships with the schools prior to seeking support for outreach programs. Most universities were already engaged in outreach activities and sought additional funding to expand the scope of their programs or to explore another dimension of outreach. A few of the programs we visited resulted from K–12 teachers initiating contact with the university. In these instances, science teachers who were aware of the lack of science resources at their schools made efforts to contact and work with science faculty to develop outreach programs. In these programs, K–12 science teachers and committees had the responsibility of involving more schools in the outreach program.

Classroom Impacts: Teachers

K–12 classrooms are complex environments. Depending on the school type and the community, teachers have to contend with many different challenges in their efforts to enhance science instruction. For example, many of the K–12 classrooms in urban schools faced issues related to motivation to learn, limited access to resources, district policies, and other issues that can impede classroom learning. In some of the classrooms in rural communities, challenges related to English proficiency and the necessary schooling skills were also an issue. What effect do outreach programs have in such complex and challenging environments? In this subsection, we focus specifically on the impact these programs had on teachers. Many of the themes highlighted here are based on comments from teacher interviews. As shown in Table 3.1, teachers reported three main impacts: increased interaction with fellow teachers, more time spent on science instruction, and changes in teaching practices that included increased utilization of teaching tools in science instruction. Each of these impacts is significant and may potentially lead to improvement in student science learning. In this subsection, we examine each of these impacts individually, discuss its significance and define the specific features of the outreach program that accounted for the impact.

Table 3.1

Program Impacts on K–12 Teachers

Impact	Cause	Potential Outcomes
Increased collegiality among teachers	Shared experience of participating in outreach program	Proactive in science Community building Stronger support system among teachers Build leadership capabilities
Increased time on science instruction	More familiar and comfortable with science as a discipline Support and weekly presence of university science students in classroom	Develop proficiency in science teaching
Utilized more teaching tools in science instruction	Access to resources from university Improved conceptual understanding of science, Observing grad and undergrad students with K–12 students Increased classroom manageability	Ability to craft lesson plans more appropriate to student needs

Increased Collegiality Among Teachers

Many of the teachers we interviewed found the increased collegiality and interaction invaluable. In fact, this was frequently one of the first things mentioned when discussing impacts of the program. From urban classrooms to suburban and affluent private schools, all teachers commented on increased collegiality as a major benefit of the programs. Most of the programs, through their professional development component, provided time for teachers to discuss what they have learned, talk about different aspects of teaching, and share information. The experience changed the way they viewed themselves as teachers, as well as using other teachers as resources. This sharing of information among teachers assisted with community building and many teachers felt that this collegiality would remain with them long after the programs were over.

The importance of this collegiality cannot be overstated. Many respondents described K–12 classrooms as environments in which teachers carried out their daily activities without much discussion or collaboration with other teachers. As one teacher describes the isolation in teaching:

> It's a killer, man . . . it's one of the worst cultural things going on, because it becomes acceptable to many of the teachers. I know I rule my roost and anything else out there I'll deal with if I have to.

Breaking down the classroom isolation and fostering interaction among teachers also contributed to developing the culture of teachers as professionals. Teachers were often amazed at the differences interactions made. One program coordinator, who had formerly worked as an elementary school teacher, explained to us that

> teachers don't really get a chance to get out of the classroom, and when they get out and interact with one another, it's like social time for them. They have so much information, and if you give them a chance to speak, they have so much to offer! They simply weren't used to being out of the classroom and treated like a professional.

We wanted to find out how outreach programs contributed to this increased collegiality and asked teachers to explain this impact. Most teachers stated that the shared experience of being involved in the outreach program provided them with a basis for communication about science teaching and learning. As a result of this experience, some teachers reported that they have become more proactive about efforts to improve science education in their schools.

Teachers Spend More Time on Science Instruction

All the teachers we interviewed stated that they spent more time on science instruction as a result of participating in the outreach program. This impact is particularly significant because conversations with teachers indicated that in many schools science receives very little attention, if any at all. One of the more common reasons for this was the limited school budget for purchasing science materials:

> A lot of teachers didn't do science before [program x] because the school wouldn't provide money for resources. Science gets put on the back burner, and not having materials makes it easy to push back.

At the elementary grade levels, science received little attention because many school districts do not have standardized tests in science prior to 5th grade. Consequently, there are few incentives for teaching science at the elementary grade levels. One program director we spoke to referred to this as a crisis:

> I can tell you that, nationwide, science is not really being taught. And right now we are in a crisis period because there is a big shift to language acquisition, and many of our states are trying not to teach science at all until the 5th grade, not even pretend to.

Teachers and the graduate students involved in direct classroom support also shared similar comments about the lack of science instruction in elementary grade levels:

I know in elementary school it's different from high school where they actually change classes. So a teacher in elementary school, if one day they didn't feel the need to do science, they could just skip it. But by having us [graduate and undergrad students], on that particular day the students are guaranteed to have their science lecture.

When you look at the elementary school levels, when children do not have the inquiry experience, they lag behind in the upper level. Many times I've heard middle and high school teachers talk about the gap in science education and it really can take place in elementary education.

In addition to lacking resources for science instruction and having few external incentives for teaching science, simply not being comfortable with the scientific subject matter also made it easy to spend less time on science than on other subjects. With such strong disincentives for teaching science, it is important that teachers be comfortable with the subject matter and understand and appreciate the importance of teaching science. Consequently, one of the important aspects of the outreach programs was the focus on changing teachers' attitudes toward science through professional development activities designed to increase science content knowledge. Many of the program directors we spoke with acknowledged the importance of getting teachers more comfortable with teaching science:

Having the teachers know more science content is a big piece because so many elementary teachers have not been provided with the science content and the accompanying pedagogy for teaching science. They don't have the science content background, and it's been very scary for the teachers. So they put the science last or put it to the side. So this program has made the teachers more comfortable and able to teach it more effectively.

Teachers were very fearful of any kind of science. Before you could get into any kind of mechanics, you have to address the concerns that teachers had regarding their fears. Give icebreaker activities, demonstrate that everything is science, e.g., soaking up water with sponge–saturation, etc.

In programs where graduate students provided classroom support, observing and working with them in the classroom helped teachers feel comfortable and more at ease with teaching science:

At first teachers admitted they didn't like science, they were afraid to teach it, but when they saw the college students in the classroom doing it, they began to enjoy it themselves. There is still some resistance out there, but there is still some evidence that shows that there is more science teaching.

Instructional Practices Include More Hands-On, Investigative Learning

Perhaps the largest reported impact of all was in the area of teaching practice. As stated in Section 2, the goals of all of the programs included enhancing science instruction, which usually meant promoting the use of hands-on instructional practices in the classroom. Thus, as a result of participating in the programs, all teachers said they used more project-based and investigational learning techniques to explain scientific concepts:

> The inquiry method is a method that really lends itself to helping children build ideas based on discovery. It's a great skill to use in all the subject areas. And I find that, personally, I use it more, the questioning technique more, instead of the traditional method of giving more information.

> Before, I taught genetics using the paper and pencil model. Now I incorporate plants in the classroom; we do hands on; the students keep a journal; and changes in curriculum are based on conversations about what was successful and what worked. In addition, the kids have fun!

For the most part, teachers welcomed the use of different teaching approaches in the classroom. Teachers acknowledged feeling limited by using only traditional, textbook-based teaching practices. Yet, prior to participating in outreach programs, many teachers felt they did have the tools at their disposal to change teaching practice. The opportunity to use new methods that included curriculum materials developed specifically for inquiry-based approaches to teaching science was very appealing to teachers:

> The information they introduced to us was so exciting because it touched something in me as a teacher. I never thought I could make such an impact on the students. I always knew that the children loved the hands-on approach. They love to be involved. So learning how to implement this formally was great! It really gave me an excitement that I could see myself going back into the classroom and sharing this with the students.

Some of the graduate students we interviewed also commented on the change in teaching practices:

> Before I came, the teacher was teaching very discontinuously and teaching to the test. Once we started working together, she cared less about SAT-9 and felt that the kids were now getting more out of the curriculum with a continuous structure.

Having the needed materials was certainly an important part of changing teaching practices for many teachers; however, having graduate and undergraduate science students in the classroom to support these changes made the difference between teachers understanding the importance of hands-on teaching methods and actually implementing these practices in the classroom on a consistent basis. As one teacher explained,

> Having access to resources, these are the kinds of things that you cannot put a price tag on. However, unless you know how to use the devices, and unless you feel safe that, if you make a mistake, there is someone who can help you, you are not going to use the equipment.

Many of the teachers' comments suggest that the graduate students served as catalysts for changing teaching practices in the classroom. The outreach programs were already infusing the schools with resources and professional development opportunities for the teachers and building the infrastructure for long-term sustainable change. However, as true catalysts, the graduate students were able to expedite a process that might have occurred on its own but might have taken much longer.

Graduate and Undergraduate Students Support Changes in Teacher Practices in a Variety of Ways

The specific ways in which the graduate students supported teachers in their efforts to change teaching practices depended primarily on the program approach. For example, in remote classroom enhancement programs, graduate students provided science content to support the teachers and students so that classroom lessons would not necessarily be limited to the teacher's knowledge. In this way, teachers could engage in more creative lesson plans without being concerned about their ability to answer technically difficult questions:

> I use this [program x] for questions that come up from kids that would be better answered by experts than by myself. I am using it as a resource for information rather than as a teaching tool. However, it is my plan to include it this year as a teaching element, to help students to think more about the process of formulating questions.

As developers of instructional materials, teachers reported that the role graduate and undergraduate students played in building and maintaining science kits for K–12 classrooms was a key part of changing teaching practice. In one program, undergraduate students design, build, and maintain circuit boards for physics instruction. They also work with the program director to develop a worksheet to guide the curriculum. The convenience of having the boards designed and managed by the students meant that teachers were more likely to use these kits in their instruction. Moreover, having access to resources that are not commonly available to teachers played an important role in changing teaching practice:

> If something breaks down I can e-mail them and say this unit does not work because I need this part, and they will mail it to me. Because of a

> limited budget, this would be difficult for me to do otherwise. From a budgeting standpoint, I can never get ahead to buy something new; here, there's no cost.

So here again, the program not only provides teachers with the resource (in this case, circuit boards) to change teaching practice but also providing them with the means to support using the additional resources (e.g., undergraduate students).

In teacher-researcher programs, we found a similar pattern. These summer programs focused on giving teachers an understanding of the scientific process so that they would be more adept at teaching the hands-on inquiry model in the fall. Additionally, the teachers also received kits and were shown different techniques that they could take back with them to the classroom. Here, one of the major impacts the graduate students had on changing teaching practice was the fact that they remained a resource for the teacher long after the completion of the program, answering questions and helping with the classroom materials.

By design, direct classroom enhancement programs gave science students the greatest opportunity to support teachers in their efforts to change teaching practices. For some teachers we interviewed, teaching practices were closely linked to classroom management issues, and science students in the classroom were an important resource for keeping the student-to-teacher ratio low enough to allow effective hands-on learning:

> The smaller student-teacher ratio is the key. With another graduate or undergraduate student in the classroom, the ratio is 15 to 1. Also, the additional knowledge base of the students helps. Smaller groups, small class sizes, means the quality of interaction with the K–12 students increases.

> The student behavior is out of hand, and the scores don't improve. Smaller class size is directly related to better grades. Having more than one person in the classroom helps the supervision and makes the student-teacher ratio smaller.

The importance of having a smaller student-to-teacher ratio for hands-on learning was apparent to the graduate students as well. When asked about recommendations for improving these programs, many graduate students suggested the number of university students coming to the classrooms be increased because too often "the K–12 students don't get enough attention."

Many of the comments from this section suggest that attempts to change teacher practice without a clear understanding of the necessary support mechanisms are bound to be short lived. Many teachers commented that mandates for changing teacher practice in science education were unrealistic because they reflected a lack of understanding about classroom environments in today's schools. And although many teachers agreed that most of these reforms were pedagogically sound and would perhaps improve science learning, these reforms were virtually impossible to carry out in a real world classroom environment. The feature that teachers liked and appreciated most about the outreach programs is that, in addition to showing them how to change teaching practices and giving them the necessary information to change teaching practice, the programs directly supported teachers' efforts to change teaching practice.

Classroom Impacts: K–12 Students

The impact of these programs on K–12 students was much more difficult to gauge. We did not interview K–12 students, so we relied on teachers' and program directors' comments to determine the impacts these programs had on the students. As shown in Table 3.2, three main impacts were commonly cited: students showed increased enthusiasm for and interest in science; the ability to engage different levels of students in science activities increased; and awareness of university culture increased. Comments from the previous section suggest that many of the impacts were probably due to the changes in teaching practice the outreach programs promoted. However, as we will see next, science students contributed to these impacts in an important way by serving as role models and mentors and by providing tangible examples of scientists for many students.

Students Demonstrate Increased Enthusiasm for and Interest in Science

The interest and the enthusiasm that students display toward science was one of the most cited impacts that the teachers reported. This impact seemed to be particularly significant in urban schools, where getting kids motivated to learn can be a challenge:

> The pedagogy is one that excites African-American children. In general, research shows that African-American kids have more interest if taught in a hands-on way and done with collaborative learning. You get kids who come to school without the specific vocabulary words but can experience success. Teachers have told us that the slowest reader in the class can be the first to get the light bulb to light up.

> The grades don't reflect it. But it does put science in a positive light; science is now seen as fun; there is more interest and the kids look forward to doing it. It hasn't improved standardized test scores; however, I would not give up on the program. Working with at-risk kids; kids lack the motivation, and this is a challenge.

Table 3.2

Program Impacts on K–12 Students

Impact	Cause	Potential outcomes
Increased enthusiasm and interest in science	Hands-on pedagogy Interaction with graduate and undergraduate science students	Enhanced science learning
Increased levels of student engagement in science activities	Hands-on pedagogy Smaller classes	Enhanced science learning
Increased awareness of university culture	Interaction with graduate and undergraduate science students	Increased awareness of different educational opportunities

Students at All Levels Are Engaged in Science Activities

Teachers felt strongly that the ability to engage all of their students in the learning process was an important classroom impact. The hands-on teaching practices promoted by the outreach programs gave students an opportunity to explore learning for themselves. More importantly though, these practices allowed *all* students to gain something from the learning experience. Despite the different learning levels in a classroom, students at all levels had the opportunity to be fully engaged in the science learning process:

> For the higher-level students, they enjoy the hands on but they would succeed either way. It's the middle- and lower-level students that are benefiting from the hands on because they are a different type of learner—maybe they are a kinesthetic learner. By doing hands on, first of all, they are going slower, so they are able to absorb the information and become an active learner and do their own exploration. But also, the real low-level learners are actually doing something. They are not lost, they are actually engaged.

> It's a hands-on program, which can be a minds-off program. Simply manipulating doesn't mean you understand, but it does give children concrete objects, and we know from cognitive research that the need for the physical is so imperative, and so they are experiencing and working with the physical as they work with more abstract issues.

> Students like it because they can see something tangible. They can explore this and come to an answer. Even if they are not getting the concepts, they can see a result and actually I find that my worst students are the first ones to the get the lights to go on and the buzzer to go off. So there's a shift of which students are finding success first, which I think helps a lot of the students.

These comments reflect what many teachers felt was an important component of the hands-on practices: providing a multidimensional aspect to learning science such that students with different learning styles could participate in the classroom activities. Moreover, most teachers felt that they still had considerable freedom to tailor the instruction to fit the level of the most of the students:

> Your students may not have the vocabulary for the kit right away so that may be a group that I may have to do a little bit more textbook first. We can at least build vocabulary because if I'm talking about glucose you need to know what glucose is, so that I can bring in the kit after I introduce it. So it just depends on your students. With my students, I really like to do the vocabulary first and then come back and reinforce the kits.

> Children can really do inquiry and gain understanding with each concept as it builds on to itself. Then what I find to be beneficial after the kits is to do more paper and pencil work on that same topic because then they have the conceptual framework that they have built from experience with materials and with concepts and understanding and investigating on their own, so that the information will become more of their own. Then I wouldn't want to leave it there because we are a testing society, plus they really need to be able to build on the information that they have using books, Internet, and technology.

Teachers however, also acknowledged that engaging students was not enough. Increasing student motivation about science, while crucial, is still just the first step. More has to be done to translate these impacts into measurable gains on student achievement tests:

> I think the program enhances science learning. But we have to move to another level. For example, the teacher will say the kids are excited about the science, but I gave him a test, and he failed. Well, he probably failed because he couldn't read well. So, we have to make improvements in the teaching to leave the content in. I still think we have a ways to go with our teacher training and getting our students to carry the lesson beyond the classroom.

Many of the Impacts Are Enhanced by Interactions with Graduate and Undergraduate Students

Although many of the impacts that the teachers describe appear to be due to changes in teaching practice, it was clear that the interaction with graduate students made a significant impact on the students as well. For example, despite differences in program approach, many teachers reported that their students worked much harder at their classroom tasks and really wanted to impress the graduate and undergraduate students:

> When they know that the audience is not the teacher, even if it's going on a
> Web page that may show up on the Internet, they will stop and try to spell
> it right or try and make it sound better, whereas they will turn in any junk
> to the teacher.

The impact of having someone else involved with the classroom was difficult to describe, yet teachers and program directors alike were aware of this added dimension:

> It's not only the pedagogy, but it's the college students as well who go in
> and the impact of the college student is one that is intangible, but you see
> how the elementary kids light up when the college students come into the
> classroom.

Certainly one aspect of this impact was that, for many of the K–12 students, the undergraduate and graduate students were seen as role models:

> The college age students are close to being big brothers and sisters to the
> kids, so that it provides a beautiful exchange for the students, and many of
> them grow close to the science students. Especially when they start out as
> freshman, they follow the students. In an urban environment, that's really
> important, the role-model link.

> Having someone in college going to teach elementary school—when I first
> went in they were like "Wow! You're in college!" They thought it was so
> incredible.

> The students were able to take the lesson a step further in terms of their
> knowledge. They were also role models. My kids weren't science oriented,
> so the science students were like role models. The kids would jump for joy
> when they came in the classroom.

Overall, the students displayed more interest in science and science careers as a result of interacting with the graduate and undergraduate students. This was also linked to a greater awareness of the possibility of attending a college or university, which may have been outside of their intended goals. As one program director explained:

> We've done some classes where the high school kids mix with the
> university kids. And the high school students see that it's not impossible
> that they might come here. They think they may go to a community
> college, but they come and they see that it's hard but not impossible, and
> they begin to see that these people are not much different than them.

Impacts on Improved Science Learning Are Difficult to Measure

Given the list of impacts discussed in the previous sections, were teachers and program directors able to see any of the potential outcomes listed in Table 3.1? Only a few of the teachers and program directors we interviewed could point to any measurable changes in test scores or grades to demonstrate increased science learning. However, both groups of interviewees were convinced that the students benefited tremendously from these programs, particularly from the changes in teaching practice that these programs produced. Yet, the evidence for improved learning was largely anecdotal. When asked specifically to point to evidence that would substantiate the claim of improved student learning, most teachers reported that students were able to recall and remember details from science experiments. Program directors were a bit more cautious in their statements and contrasted it with the situation prior to outreach:

> I know that even if the kits are not being used as we hoped them to and if the teachers aren't as wonderful as we would like, no matter what negatives we might put on it, it is better than what was happening four years ago. I know that all of what goes on in the classrooms is not superlative, but I know it is better than what was going on before this program.

For many that we spoke to, this seemed to be an all-too-common dilemma of outreach programs—the "we know it's a good thing, but how do we show it?" syndrome. There were two main responses to the question of why programs were unable to demonstrate quantitative evidence of improved science learning. The first reason had to do with time. Comments from program directors and coordinators reflected the view that expecting to see student achievement gains in less than five years is unrealistic, particularly when only a few of the variables (e.g., professional development of teachers) related to low student achievement in science have been attended to:

> There's a long time lag between implementation of a program and a measurable student outcome, and so this time window has been too short. Implementation of a program that's primarily focused on professional development for teachers is a necessary condition for student achievement, but I don't think it's a sufficient condition for school achievement. So I think we would be remiss if we say that this particular effort is going to have a marked difference in student achievement if we don't attend to the other factors underlying the causes of low student achievement to begin with.

> Change is not immediate. This was not designed as a research program, but as an intervention, a more ephemeral, Byzantine process.

The second reason that was often given had to do with limited budgets that did not allow an opportunity to plan evaluations that could inform directors and coordinators on how best to refine programs in ways that might lead to improvements in student achievement:

> What I have been able to perceive as a flaw in our design is that we have not been able to do the plan, do, check, and act cycle. We've been doing a

lot of planning and a lot of doing, but we've not been given the
opportunity, either because at first we weren't allowed to go into the
schools, or later when the program was too big, we didn't have the people
to really be in the schools and know what's happening. So, we had to go on
faith or on what we heard, but we didn't really have that information that
we wished we now had.

Challenges Faced by K–12 Schools and Communities

An important piece of this discussion on impacts is an understanding of the
challenges outreach programs faced in their efforts to improve science learning.
In the absence of understanding the challenges, it is difficult to put the impacts
listed in the previous sections in perspective. We asked program participants to
comment on the challenges they experienced participating in outreach programs.
In this section, we list those challenges that were based on policies or practices
related to K–12 schools.

Outreach Programs Targeting Schools in Underserved Communities Face Unique Challenges

Clearly, the biggest challenges for outreach programs in urban schools were
issues surrounding the motivation to learn. Teachers and program directors alike
all commented on the difficulties associated with establishing outreach programs
in schools where improving science learning was often lost amidst deeper
classroom challenges:

> There are many kids coming into the public school systems today that
> don't have a desire to learn, and I don't care what kind of content you put
> in front of them, if you don't deal with that issue you're not going to make
> the impact you are trying to make.

> You are dealing with these poor kids who have no real interest in
> education, and you've got to do something to get them interested. If I were
> a teacher in that setting, my enthusiasm would drop off exponentially. The
> environment is very difficult.

Programs doing outreach to schools in rural communities faced additional
challenges in efforts to enhance science instruction. In these schools, the student
population is highly transient, and a number of the students come from migrant
families. One teacher commented on his class:

> I have a fair amount of ESL {English as a Second Language] kids that have
> the motivation but not the English skills, in some cases not the schooling
> skills, having come from farmworking.

These comments highlight why teachers were so encouraged by what they saw occurring in the classroom as a result of these outreach programs. Here you have schools with students that are not interested in being in class, perhaps with insufficient skills to be in class, and yet according to the teachers, they are much more engaged and excited about learning science. These comments are also important in considering the ability of evaluation to measure all the dimensions of outreach programs and the ways they impact student learning.

Other challenges were related to how the expertise of graduate and undergraduate students was utilized in the classroom. Rather than being content resources, some graduate students were expected to do most of the teaching, or in other instances, they served primarily as extra sets of hands to aid teachers in setting up science equipment. One program coordinator noted that, in some classrooms, teachers allow the students to do most of the teaching:

> A lot of teachers go limp in the classroom and just let the science students take over. The teachers see this as cognitive checkout time. This is what we were afraid of, that the teachers would see this as free time and would expect our students to come in and do it for them.

> Frankly, I think one of the biggest things this program has done is provide an extra set of hands and brains. The original model was that somehow these undergraduates would be a resource of information somehow, and it's not that way. They are resources for dealing with classroom, helping to prepare materials, testing out labs, etc. The original model is not what is happening at all.

These examples suggest that achieving a balance between teacher needs and university ideas of what teachers need is difficult. These partnerships are important because they offer the opportunity to infuse classrooms with ideas and resources that may not be available otherwise. However, if these ideas and resources are not meeting the real "teacher needs," programs like this run the risk of having their resources used out of context. The previous examples suggest that the real teacher need may be smaller classes, not necessarily content experts in the classroom. In this situation, it is highly likely that the university student who works in the classroom may primarily work in a teachers aide capacity. Similarly, if a teacher feels that his or her background in science is inadequate to teach certain topics, it is likely that a graduate student will be asked to do much of the classroom teaching.

District Policies That Focus on Improving Math and Reading Skills Leave Little Time for Science

All of the schools reported district policies as one of major challenges they faced in participating in science outreach programs. Most teachers and program directors felt that district policies were often in conflict with the goals of the outreach program. For some schools, the district's focus on improving test scores meant devoting more classroom time to improving math and reading skills, which left little time for science:

> The new superintendent has said we have children who cannot read at grade level, and that will be our focus. So teachers are saying "You have to do 3 hours of reading, do some math, and that's it for the day." So if the kids just do reading and math, then there's not likely to be an increase in their science achievement.

> So much time is spent in reading, and maybe they do science once a week. Reading is the priority. I think many people are afraid of the science because it is such an unknown.

Moreover, many of the comments revealed that during "test time" very little time, if any, is spent on science instruction. In preparation for standardized tests, school instruction focuses almost entirely on math and reading, and it is difficult to maintain the consistency of science instruction that had been built up over the months:

> All instruction stops in February, and it's skill and drill, practice for test all day long. It doesn't necessarily mean that they are going to do any better. So the focus is on math and reading. And only at a few grade levels is science tested. So it's at those grade levels that the teachers focus more on science, but it's a problem because it is supposed to be a cumulative test and so you can't teach it all in 3rd or 5th grade. So the teachers will say that the tests focus on Math and English, and that's how we get our pay increases because if our students do better on ITBS [Iowa Test of Basic Skills], we get merit pay.

> The teachers don't want the university students in the classroom during test time, and if they are in there, they want them to help them prepare for the test. Our program was shut down six weeks before the Iowa Test of Basic Skills.

> In general, science is low on the totem pole, science and science education. Especially when faced [with] pressure for literacy and math, science gets pushed back. ETS [Educational Testing Service] needs to start adding science to tests or it will be pushed down.

This challenge seemed to be particularly acute for outreach programs that partnered with urban schools. Moreover, these comments reflect how the focus on improving test scores and the incentive of merit-based pay can undermine efforts to improve science education, particularly since science is often not a focus of many state and district testing policies.

Strong District Leadership Is Needed to Support Changes in Science Curriculum

It is important that districts be aware of and support the necessary changes in classrooms that occur as a result of inquiry-based practices. Many of these inquiry-based approaches bring a different method of teaching into the classroom, a teaching style that encourages students to explore their own questions, and require a certain amount of freedom in the classroom. In many urban schools, classroom management is of paramount importance. Principals that observe what appears to be mayhem in the classroom may judge a teacher's performance harshly. One teacher commented:

> My principal is a stickler for discipline, and if he comes to my room and I have these kids in small groups and all this noise, I'm going to have problems with my rating.

Strong district support is also needed to stand up to parents who may not understand or who oppose some of the changes created by reform. One program director describes the impact of not having strong district support for the use of kits:

> Most parents have been taught through textbooks, and they want the children taught the same way. And the previous superintendent was very political. He pretty much told us that the kits are much better than the textbooks, but the parents want the textbooks. And that was disappointing to me because the superintendent should be leading the charge. He should be telling them that these textbooks are not the way to be going for the new century. And if he catches some flack for it, so what. But he was going to be expedient. So if the parents wanted textbooks and yelled loud enough, whether the kids learned or not was secondary.

Concluding Thoughts

Outreach programs affected K–12 schools in many different ways. Comments from teachers and program directors indicated that these programs had the following impacts:

- increased the science content knowledge in the classrooms
- supported changes in teacher instructional practices
- increased collegiality among teachers

- provided needed resources and materials for science instruction
- motivated many K–12 students to take an interest in science.

Science graduate and undergraduate students played a key role in these programs by providing the resources and support necessary to promote changes in teacher's instructional practices *and* attitudes toward teaching science. Although many of the reforms in science education provide clear goals and objectives for what science ought to look like, they provide little indication of how to get there (Clune et al., 1997). Without a road map or a clear indication of the path to implementation, it is easy for many teachers to falter, devise the curriculum based on a limited understanding of science, or revert to more comfortable and familiar ways of teaching science. Thus, outreach programs that utilize university students may be useful in bridging the gap between current practices in science education and practices that are aligned with the recommendations of the science standards.

The multidimensional nature of the support the university students provided was a key ingredient in facilitating some of the impacts that were identified. The teachers were able to draw on the science students' ability to provide expertise in science content, to support teachers' learning of new scientific techniques, and to serve as role models and motivators for the K–12 students. This versatility meant that science graduate and undergraduate students could specifically provide the type of support teachers needed to implement changes in classrooms. And even though these changes might have occurred anyway over the long run, time is a precious commodity that many students are not given enough of, particularly students in urban schools. For each year of incremental progress toward changing teacher attitudes and gradually changing teacher practices, a generation of students may be losing opportunities to develop the solid foundation in math and science necessary to contribute to a society that has become increasingly scientifically and technologically based.

For some programs, it was difficult to distinguish the impacts due to the science students from those that were due to other resources provided by the outreach program. For example, it may be that simply combining increased time with specific content improves student learning. Even in these instances, it can be argued that simply facilitating these opportunities to learn made the science students a meaningful part of the impact. Clearly, one of the future research issues that emerges from these findings is the need to determine which efforts truly require the input of science graduate and undergraduate students. Science graduate students, in particular, are a critical part of the research university, and it is important for programs to be able to effectively utilize the skills and talents these students bring to K–12 schools. Future research designed to look at this issue might compare classrooms having teachers' aides with classrooms having science students as one way to gauge the impact of science students in the classroom.

Another important issue for future research is how to measure the impacts of these programs. The findings in this section provide an important starting point for considering and developing the types of metrics that could be used to evaluate the impacts of these programs. The information presented here highlights the variety of impacts these programs had on both teachers and students and suggests that multiple metrics are needed to assess the impacts of the programs fully. Moreover, the usual metrics for evaluation, such as an increase in math or science test scores, may not be the most significant or the most appropriate outcomes to expect from these programs. Interviewee comments suggest that some of the greatest impacts were the attitudinal changes the programs fostered toward science. One may well argue that these sorts of changes are needed before meaningful changes in teaching practice can take place. Assessments geared toward detecting or measuring the changes in attitudes toward science on the part of teachers and students may be one way to evaluate the impacts of such programs (see, for example, NSF, 1998). Other assessments could focus on skills that combine scientific process knowledge with scientific content knowledge. For example, teachers were eager to share stories about students' ability to retain detailed information about different science activities and their increased curiosity and interest in science topics. Exploration, explanation, description and observation are all critical components of inquiry-based approaches to science.[1] Thus, tests could be developed that evaluate the scientific sophistication of students' questions or the level of detail used to describe different phenomena.

The comments in this section also suggest that examining the impacts on teachers is equally important for full program assessment. Since much of the focus is on changing teacher practices and teacher attitudes, an important metric might be to examine or look for increased confidence and competency in teaching science. School-level changes might be another metric for evaluation. For example, is there increased collaboration and discussion among teachers as a result of the programs? Are teachers continuing to spend more time on science instruction, and are they learning how to tailor science instruction to the needs of their students?

---

[1]See Kahle (1998) for a discussion of different sorts of indicators that can be used to assess the quality of different science and math reforms.

It is a long path from implementing reform-based practices in the classroom to demonstrating improved student learning. Along the way, it is important to have resources that help teachers and students remain on the path. The outreach programs and the science students that participate in them may be invaluable resources for this process. Moreover, these programs might serve as catalysts to facilitate the alignment of certain pieces of the reform to allow more-focused measures toward improved student leaning in science to be successful.

4. Outreach Programs: The Perspective from Institutions of Higher Education

This section tackles the question of higher-education impacts by examining the perspectives of the science graduate and undergraduate students, program directors, coordinators and managers that participated in these eight outreach programs. As Section 3 showed, outreach programs that link universities and schools offer numerous benefits to K–12 classrooms in the form of classroom support from graduate and undergraduate students, instructional resources, and curriculum assistance. This section examines the other side of the partnership and asks what impacts these programs have on institutions of higher education, and more specifically what do universities, and science departments in particular, gain through partnerships with K–12 classrooms. Do these outreach programs provide more than a warm, fuzzy feeling? The answers to these questions are critical because, although most outreach programs are designed to be partnerships, few actually attain this goal. Often, outreach programs that link universities and K–12 schools are implemented with the assumption that the primary benefits are unidirectional, flowing from universities to K–12 classrooms. However, a broader question is how much of this unidirectionality is embedded in the structure of outreach programs. Certainly, the primary purpose of most outreach programs is to support the improvement of K–12 education, but few programs evolve to the level of equal knowledge-sharing among the participants. Moreover, analysis of the impacts on institutions of higher education is often neglected; as a result, few programs are designed in ways that can maximize the positive attributes of the programs for both institutions of higher education and K–12 schools.

This section follows a structure similar to that of Section 3. It begins with a description of the universities and how the outreach programs are structured within them. The following subsection (and here we depart from the pattern of the previous section) discusses the motives for participation among graduate and undergraduate students, program directors, coordinators, and managers. We felt this discussion was important to include for a number of reasons. Participation in outreach programs is voluntary for many of the higher-education participants, and identifying the motives for participation may reveal important clues about the success and effectiveness of programs. Also, the reasons for participation for many program directors and managers were linked to the impacts they wanted the programs to have, so we thought it was useful to identify them.

Following the material on motives, we discuss the program impacts. Many of the university students we spoke with were either currently participating in one of these programs or had just completed work with one, and their comments reflect immediate, short-term impacts. Interviews with program directors and managers whose participation in these programs spanned a number of years provided insights into some of the broader, long-term impacts of these programs. The comments from the program directors and managers are important here because they link the impacts in this section to strategies for long-term program outcomes. We conclude by discussing whether the impacts identified can be formalized as program goals for participants from the higher-education culture. Do these programs offer significant benefits that can be expanded on? Or do these programs pose other problems—such as increasing time-to-degree for graduate students or recruitment and retention problems that might undermine the success of these programs? As we will discuss further in Section 5, the answers to these questions are a critical link to program sustainability.

Sponsoring Universities and Outreach Program Structure

All of the graduate and undergraduate students we interviewed attended Research I universities. According to the Carnegie Classification of Institutions of Higher Education, institutions of this type offer a full range of baccalaureate programs, are committed to graduate education through the doctorate, and give high priority to research. They award 50 or more doctoral degrees each year. In addition, they receive $40 million or more in federal support annually. Graduate students play an important role in Research I universities and represent a valuable workforce for the university. The emphasis on research in these universities often means that faculty members in the sciences spend a majority of their time engaged in research, while graduate students contribute greatly to the teaching of the undergraduate students. This is particularly true for many of the science courses, where most graduate students usually support themselves for part of their tenure on stipends received as teaching assistants.

For most of the programs we examined, grants for the outreach program were awarded to the university, and the principal investigator of the grant was usually a full-time professor within the science department. Because of the educational nature of these awards, collaborations between science department and school of education faculty were frequent. For example, in one program, the educational outreach component was a small piece of a much larger grant to the science department. As such, primary responsibility for the educational component was handed over to faculty within the school of education. The responsibilities included setting up and structuring the program and recruiting science students. Although science faculty members were aware of the educational component of the grant, their responsibility for ensuring its success was minimal. Other models of collaborations usually involved a senior faculty member in the science department working with school of education personnel. In these instances, recruitment of graduate and undergraduate students often fell to a single member of the science faculty, and other parts of the program, such as pedagogical training, were the responsibility of school of education staff.

Motivation for Participation in Outreach Programs: Graduate and Undergraduate Students

With the exception of the students in the teacher-preparation program, all of the graduate students we interviewed intended to pursue research careers, either in academia or industry. Similarly, the undergraduates were also on a professional track, with plans to attend medical school or graduate school in a scientific discipline. So, in the absence of a practical consideration, such as preparation for teaching careers, why did the opportunity to go into K–12 classrooms or work with K–12 teachers appeal to many of them? Interviews with undergraduate and graduate students indicated one or more of the following four motivations:

- the opportunity to use their science knowledge in a broader context
- the experience and challenge of interacting with a different population
- improvement in communication skills
- the sizable compensations that some programs offered.

The opportunity to use science knowledge to make a difference in the schools and the surrounding communities was one of the most frequently cited motives. Working beyond the laboratory and having real-world impacts was an important component of outreach programs:

> I was working in a lab. I didn't like it; it didn't connect me to the outside world, and I was looking for other options to interact science with the real world, and I really liked it.

> I could go to school and come to classes, and that's just for my benefit, but the benefit for me is helping other people out. It's a worthwhile cause. I have a general interest in science; it's helping children, and I think that's important.

Graduate students, who usually worked as teaching assistants for undergraduate courses, found the experience and challenge of interacting with another population to be particularly attractive:

> I was told about the program by the vice chairman. In the graduate chemistry department we have to cover our stipend some way, so this fulfilled that requirement and provided me an option to help within the community, which is something I wanted to do.

> I wasn't too thrilled about interacting with another group of undergraduates, and the thought of having a different student population as a teaching requirement was something that appealed to me.

Some science faculty were surprised at the value their students placed on outreach, expecting students on professional career tracks to be more interested in programs more aligned with their career goals:

> I was not sensitive to how interested undergraduates are in doing this! For example, I was amazed at these two students, both premed students that have no long-term interest in education, but they had enough interest to work with me a whole semester without any obvious payoff in terms of their career.

On the more pragmatic side, many students believed that participation in these outreach programs would help them improve their communication skills. Moreover, communicating effectively with a broader audience was thought to be an important skill for scientists:

> For me it was sort of a selfish sort of thing, to get better at communicating science because I realized I wasn't particularly good at communicating with nonscientists, and I wanted to get the experience of being able to do that.

> I think scientists have an obligation to explain science to the general public because the people who you are educating will be making decisions about funding science and will be doing things like sitting on juries, evaluating scientific information. So, I think informing the citizenry about science and making it less scary is an important role for scientists to fulfill.

Some of the programs offered sizable compensatory packages; however, none of the graduate students cited these as incentives or reasons for participation. Although it is difficult to assess the degree to which the compensation attracted students to participate in outreach programs, it seems fair to conclude that none of the graduate students we interviewed were doing it solely for the money.

On the other hand, for programs that utilized undergraduate students, compensation played an important role. It ensured their continued participation in the program and guaranteed some level of consistent, responsible behavior on the part of the students. One program coordinator noted the importance of providing stipends for undergraduate students:

> The other piece that has to be considered is that this program pays the students, so there is a greater incentive for them to be present. So they are responsible in a different way than volunteers. We found that, with the undergraduates they are very apt not to show up. Even if they are enthusiastic and want to do, there is something missing in the follow-up.

Undergraduate students in the teacher-preparation program also cited stipends as one major reason they were attracted to the teacher-preparation program. Some undergraduate mathematics majors explained to us that the amount of the stipend was a key reason for interest in teacher-preparation programs:

> I thought what was great about coming here was knowing that I can get paid, get a stipend for just observing teachers and stuff.[1] I put in four hours a week for a year, that's not bad for a thousand-dollar stipend a quarter.

> I knew there was money, a stipend; that interested me of course. Also, I think the reason why—if I was going to go into education, I was aware of the other programs that make you pay—I mean they make you do a whole year of student teaching. In this program, I get my master's degree and I get paid for doing this my junior and senior year.

Motivation for Participation in Outreach Programs: Program Directors, Coordinators, and Managers

Program directors, coordinators, and managers with scientific backgrounds also wanted to share science knowledge with schools and communities and valued making "real-world" impact on educational issues. Many of the program directors, coordinators, and managers we spoke with described a single incident, a point of awareness about the state of science education that mobilized them to either initiate a program or to participate in an existing one:

> My initial involvement started with a student that worked in my lab for two years. He got very excited about working in the school system, and the reason I'm involved is that he brought local high school students to look at the greenhouse. I gave them a tour of the greenhouse. I was so amazed at how little they knew—that was the stimulus! These kids knew zero, and these kids were taking high school biology!

> I noticed my grandson getting bored with science, and I went to see the principal. I told her what I was thinking and asked if I could speak to the

---

[1]The emphasis of the quote is on the importance of stipends to undergraduates. As noted, this student participated in a teacher-preparation program that required one year of teacher observation as part of training. We do not want this student's comments to leave the mistaken impression that university science students typically observed teachers rather than supported them in the classrooms.

> faculty with the idea that I would offer them this program and see if it would grow and do it as a pilot project purely on a voluntary basis.

These comments suggest that an awareness of the issues in K–12 schools can mobilize scientists to become involved in outreach activities.

We also noted a predominance of women who had completed science doctoral degrees (in some cases postdoctoral research) participating in these programs. Their comments suggested that they found a high degree of fulfillment in working at a programmatic level in outreach programs.[2]

Other program directors, managers, and coordinators cited social concerns as a primary motivating force for their involvement. Gender and equity concerns about the composition of the future workforce were two of the issues program directors viewed as critical areas that could be addressed through these programs. For example, one respondent remarked on the need to create a larger pool of minority physicians and saw achievement in math and science as one way to get there:

> The research is very clear. Students coming out of underserved populations are more likely to go back to serve, and there is evidence that minority physicians are apt to serve those populations. So I have a vested interest to see that those young students with talent, that we tap those students with potential and get them motivated so that they will not only be more excited about science, but they will also pursue health careers, careers in biomedical science, physicians, engineers in all the areas that we are underrepresented.

For other programs, social justice was a major theme and strong educational preparation in math and science was seen as a direct path to achieving this:

> It is not just good enough to be a good science teacher. We are looking for good science teachers that are committed to all kids. Most of the teachers [in our teacher-preparation program] did not come from low-income areas. So, these aren't their communities. And so, we are trying to figure out how do you get people, students of color, committed to these educational arenas to want to teach and go back to their communities?

Others felt that the needs of the surrounding community had largely been neglected and that the motivation for the program was to match the mission statement of the university:

> The president [of the university] said that this university would no longer be considered an ivory tower, an enclave surrounded by this urban

---

[2]There seems to be an untold story about the contributions of women scientists to education outreach programs. Although this is not directly related to the present work, further research may be useful in uncovering ways to tap into this resource.

community. It was critical that the university focus on the needs of the community and have community programs that matched the mission of the university.

Motives for participation played a critical role in the success of these programs. As discussed in Section 5, a common characteristic of many of the outreach programs we examined was a shared vision among programmatic staff that viewed the goals of outreach more broadly than simply improving science learning.

Impact on Graduate and Undergraduate Students

Despite the differences in the students we interviewed and the types of programs they participated in, two impacts from participating in outreach programs were often mentioned. The first had to do with the growth and knowledge of science and learning science, such as improved communication skills, reassessment of their own learning, and understanding of scientific concepts. The second had to do with the perspective students gained from participating in these programs. Many students commented on awareness of different learning styles and a greater appreciation of the skills necessary to be a teacher. In this subsection, we discuss each of these impacts and their significance in leading to outcomes for reshaping the graduate student experience. We also ask what it would take to make these impacts more substantial or more far reaching. Can a year of outreach be expected to make an impact on the experience of university science students, or is the experience of graduate and undergraduate education enhanced because of programs like this?

Interacting with K–12 Teachers and Students Causes Students to Reassess Their Own Learning and Understanding

Improved communication skills were one of the main impacts that graduate students reported. Most of them were attracted to these programs for the opportunity to communicate science to a broader audience. Perhaps what was more surprising for the graduate students was the extent to which they had to reevaluate how much they understood about the science they thought they knew. For many, the improved communications skills came as a result of having to reassess their own understanding of many scientific concepts that they had taken for granted. Many graduate students remarked on the amount of learning that takes place when one has to explain concepts to others who may not be as familiar with the scientific jargon:

> It's given me a great opportunity to teach some research. Actually, a lot of things I do, I do by rote. I know how to do them, explaining it makes me try to think about why I am doing it and what purpose it has.

> I feel that I benefit because I go back to remember things. It clarifies things for me, I realize the misconceptions I had.

> Different classrooms have different science kits. I know I don't remember a lot about different topics from my school days, so it helps me to review and present that to the class.

Many of the graduate students spent time as teaching assistants for science courses within their disciplines, but serving as a teaching assistant was, by some accounts, a very formulaic experience. However, in teaching to a broader audience, the graduate students were forced to think more deeply about things. Explaining a concept like electricity to a sixth grader, without it degenerating into equations, was a challenge for most graduate students. As a result, they were able to reassess their own learning, something being a teaching assistant did not inspire. Comments from interviewees suggested that this reassessment of learning is uniquely a function of teaching to and interacting with persons outside of the scientific community. For example, in the teacher-researcher programs, graduate students said that working with teachers forced them to think more about the core issues of the research projects they were working on. Teachers cared much more about the goals and purpose of the research rather than some of the methodological details. Teacher-researcher programs also provided the added benefit of helping the graduate students learn to manage and supervise research activities, which some graduate students viewed as an important experience:

> I am kind of thinking about going into academia at the end of this, and while TAing[3] is going to give me a lot of classroom experience, it's not going to give me a lot of experience directing other people's research.

Moreover, many graduate students themselves felt that they had more of an impact in working in K–12 classrooms than in serving as TAs in undergraduate science courses where the majority of their time would be spent "haggling over [a] 1-point grade difference with a premed major."

---

[3]"TAing" refers to the activity of working as a teaching assistant.

Partnerships with Urban Schools Provide Students with a Broader Context and Understanding of Education

Graduate and undergraduate students who supported K–12 teachers in underserved communities found that working in urban schools provided them an opportunity to see and understand the ways in which environment and resources can affect learning. When asked about their experiences in the classrooms, many students mentioned motivation to learn as one of the unique challenges they faced in supporting K–12 teachers in inner-city schools:

> If you have an undergrad at the university, the kids are looking to get the education. It's almost like force-feeding for some of the kids in the high school. They don't see anything beyond their life. The come from radically different backgrounds compared to students at the university. They don't see the point. The challenge is to actually bring them into class and make them pay attention, and show them that yes you can do science, and it isn't just for somebody else.

Despite the challenges, many students felt that their work in K–12 schools was more valuable than their work as teaching assistants in the university.

Impacts on Institutions of Higher Education

We were also interested in whether these programs had impacts beyond the graduate and undergraduate students. For example, by participating in outreach programs, did program participants feel that institutions gain more credibility in the community? Did the participation in outreach increase the number of undergraduates taking certain courses, or increase the number of majors, or diversity of students within certain departments? The answers to this question varied with the scope of the outreach program. However, most program directors felt that participation in outreach program enhanced the image of the institution in the eyes of the community. This was particularly true for institutions that had strained relations with the community or were perceived to be ivory tower enclaves, removed from the neighborhoods around them:

> The university had an isolationist approach to the community, and the only way they interacted with the community is when they wanted data from them. The schools have had a whole series of these attempts that petered out, so there is a lack of trust. Having had these experiences, the schools have learned not to depend [on the university] very much. However, enough good stuff has happened with the university in the last 5 years that they at least come to the table.

Moreover, many program directors reported that K–12 teachers took pride in their affiliation and connection with the institution and that this went a long way toward community building.

In addition to improved community relations, a few programs focused on reshaping the quality of undergraduate and graduate education in science and the role of outreach programs toward that goal:

> This program is changing the nature of outreach and adding a new dimension. It is about improving undergraduate and graduate education. It is not just another thing for the students to do. Students are affiliated and engaged in a department, designing outreach units. We are changing and improving undergraduate education, science research, and science education.

As explained by one program manager, engaging science undergraduate majors in outreach programs is good for the university. Undergraduate science core requirements typically have low approval rate among the students. Linking science courses to outreach programs, a feature that most students give high ratings at the university, may be one way to engage students and also to solve strategic community problems.

To many that we interviewed, these outreach programs clearly that offered graduate students a unique type of teaching and learning experience. Many program directors felt that these programs provided a level of in-depth learning that was important in reshaping and improving graduate education:

> If you give these grad students a hard problem from a textbook, they can do it, but they can't quite explain what that has to do with the world. Here's an opportunity for an improvement of graduate school education, and the students see the value in it. It's more than a warm fuzzy feeling. We are providing applied learning that they can tolerate.

Furthermore, some program directors believed that the experience of participating in outreach could benefit graduate students by helping them with their teaching skills. Improving the teaching skills of graduate students was also viewed as a benefit to the university, particularly when many graduate students serve as teaching assistants for undergraduate science courses. As one program coordinator summarized,

> This is a great opportunity for graduate students, providing ways that this is clearly a benefit to their teaching. Most programs like this [direct classroom support] are in the humanities and social sciences, but it is really important to explore this in the physical sciences.

Challenges Within the Universities

An important goal for most of the outreach programs was sustainability. Program directors expressed the desire to have their programs exist as an integral part of the university. Thus, in answering our questions about the challenges, respondents often referred to the challenges and obstacles linked to creating sustainable programs. Many of these challenges were based on the culture of universities, particularly of Research I universities, and their focus on research and research products as one of the most valued outcomes of the university system. This perspective created what many felt was an extremely narrow focus for graduate education, one that devalued teaching and discouraged any activities that would distract graduate students from their research and potentially increase the time-to-degree for graduate students. We next discuss some of the challenges outreach programs faced from universities, challenges that in the long run may impact their sustainability.

Lack of Support for Outreach Programs Among Science Faculty

Although many science faculty were not directly involved in these programs, their support was important. Graduate and undergraduate students often heard about these programs from departmental faculty, and so the endorsement of science faculty was important in the recruitment and sustained participation of graduates and undergraduates in these programs. Because many of the program directors, coordinators, and mangers we interviewed were also faculty within the science departments, they were able to offer insightful comments as to why many of their colleagues were not supportive of outreach programs. The reasons ranged from benign disinterest to active opposition to the fundamental concept of the outreach program itself. For example, one interviewee stated "most faculty don't want to be bothered with educational outreach because it hinders research productivity." Still other faculty were skeptical of education outreach programs and view them as having very little impact on achieving the stated goals. One of the program directors described one of the more difficult aspects of setting up the program, that of

> persuading the scientists that this was worthwhile. Although NSF mandated that there be some educational component linked to this program, it was met with cynicism on the part of the faculty. Was this anymore than political correctness? Would there be any real impact on the people that this program is designed to help? So, there was a subgroup of faculty that questioned whether this was a worthwhile activity.

Other faculty viewed the goals of outreach as being counter to the goals of the graduate program and actively opposed the participation of graduate students in the outreach programs:

> [Participation in outreach] would be discouraged by the department. It would be seen as a diversion. Graduate students are so focused on getting a Ph.D., this is not a popular alternative. We would much rather have them teach university courses, which looks good in terms of job hunting.

This sentiment was common among interviewees involved in direct classroom enhancement programs that placed graduate students in the classrooms with teachers. In fact, a combination of skepticism about the impact of outreach programs and a conviction that outreach programs using graduate students in K–12 classrooms had little long-term payoff led to the development of the one teacher-preparation program we studied. In the comment below, the program director describes the rationale that led to the creation of the program:

> I became disillusioned with the use of the money. It was difficult to get students to do this [participate in outreach]. And although, undoubtedly, they benefited the kids in the classes, it was in no way preparing people to get into high school and elementary teaching. The graduate students just used it as a way of supporting themselves. They were interested in getting a Ph.D. and going on with their research careers. And I felt we could make better use of the money.

This comment embodies the major criticism of direct classroom enhancement programs that involve graduate students: What is the long-term payoff from getting graduate students who have no interest in teaching involved in K–12 classrooms? Moreover, these comments suggest that, to get faculty to be more supportive of education outreach programs, there has to be a clearer understanding of the long-term goal. Science faculty at Research I universities are driven toward producing research and research products. Programs and activities that are not in line with that focus are perceived as liabilities. As outreach programs consider ways to get more faculty support, they may explore ways to align their programs with research productivity.

Turf Issues Between Education and Science Faculty

As mentioned earlier, many of the programs involved some form of collaboration between education and science faculty. And although, this was a positive long-term strategy, several comments suggested that bringing these two departments, who were often on different sides of the fence, together presented many challenges. Many program directors acknowledge that there are often turf issues between schools of education and the physical sciences that made it challenging for faculty from these two groups to work together. Regarding recruitment and training of university science students, the primary challenge between these two groups centered on the emphasis on content knowledge versus pedagogical training. One of the program directors explained the difference this way:

> The science community feels that education in depth, in the subject matter, is essential if the teacher is to be able to have some perspective and recognize that there are shortages in what he or she is teaching, especially in a reform context. But obviously just having the content knowledge doesn't make you a good teacher, and that goes without saying. But it's necessary. And now there is tension between people in mathematics who are involved in the program and people in education.

Other challenges centered on the involvement of preservice teachers in outreach programs. Although many education people viewed this as a logical extension of teacher-preparation programs, science faculty were reluctant to recruit students who did not have the grounding in science content:

> We have had some difficulty getting the education department to connect to what we're doing. We have some differences here. If these folks [education students] are going to be teaching anyway, then we should get them as a preservice function and get them involved. Now they may not have as much science content as a science person, but why not give them this experience. It's not a conflict, it's just a difference in emphasis.

Despite these challenges, collaboration with schools of education was critical to the success of many of these programs. In addition to providing pedagogical training for the graduate and undergraduate science students, some programs used student-teacher interns to accompany science students into classrooms as part of their training. In many instances, visible support and involvement from schools of education gave outreach programs more credibility in the eyes of the K–12 schools. One program coordinator explained the importance of collaborations with schools of education:

> The district liked that we were bringing in the School of Education also. We potentially represent not only direct resources to them, but direct resources for improving the pipeline.

Concluding Thoughts

We opened the section by asking what these programs offer universities. It seems clear that these programs offered the science graduate and undergraduate students an opportunity to reassess their learning and understanding of scientific concepts; a chance to develop better communication skills by interacting with people outside of their community; and perhaps for some, an enriching experience that gave them a different cultural sensitivity and awareness. These may be significant impacts not only for the science students also for the universities. Studies have shown that, in the universities, as in the schools, meaningful learning in science courses is limited to a few students who are headed for graduate school, while most other students including most prospective teachers get through their courses by memorization (see Anderson, 1999). To the extent that the outreach programs enrich student learning and understanding of science, undergraduates who participate in outreach may benefit from these experiences, which reinforce and challenge their knowledge of science. These programs may also increase undergraduate enrollment in science courses and may increase the number of science majors at universities.

It is more difficult to assess the significance of these impacts for graduate students. Further research would be necessary to determine whether the experience of working with K–12 schools improved their skills as teaching assistants, helped them think through and articulate their research to others, or even had long-term impacts on their ability to teach introductory science courses as future faculty. In terms of overall benefits to the university, the improved community relations seemed to be important to the program directors, and many felt that this could be used as a selling point in discussions with deans and other administrative staff about the importance of outreach.

Challenges from the higher-education culture primarily stem from the reward systems at most universities, which place high priority on scholarly research and research products. In this environment, activities that take time from research are often viewed as liabilities. Thus, outreach programs that utilize science graduate and undergraduate students, a valuable workforce in universities (particularly Research I universities) face increased scrutiny. We found this to be particularly true of the direct classroom enhancement programs. Of the different types of programs we visited, these were viewed with the most skepticism from university faculty, who were less inclined to support this method of outreach. Unlike the teacher researcher programs, which allowed graduate students to remain in the laboratory and work with teachers, direct classroom enhancement programs required graduate students to work outside the research arena and immerse themselves completely in teaching in a different culture, which had little, if anything, to do with research. Many science faculty questioned not only the purpose of these programs for K–12 schools but also the long-term impacts of these programs on the schools. While these are difficult questions to answer, they do point to some of the core issues that must be addressed if outreach programs are to be integrated into universities.

Challenges from the university also arise from some of the pedagogical issues these programs faced. Training for both science students and teachers seems to

54

be a critical component of success, particularly for the direct enhancement programs that place science students in the classrooms. Despite their intended role of support, the presence of science students in the classroom means that they are influencing learning. For this reason, training in pedagogical skills aimed at effective methods of communicating scientific concepts is crucial. Moreover, for teachers who are utilizing the content knowledge that science students bring to their classrooms, training is necessary to ensure that the teachers use this resource in the most appropriate manner. Pedagogical training would enable both K–12 students and teachers to derive the maximum benefits of having science students in the classrooms as resources. Furthermore, the science graduate and undergraduate would also benefit from coursework or training that would emphasize communication skills and methods of explaining scientific concepts. Indeed, for many science graduate students, improving communication skills was the key reason cited for participation in outreach programs and pedagogical training may serve to attract more students to these programs.

5. Summary and Conclusions

This section addresses the third research question of this study and begins with a discussion of some of the features that enabled programs to effectively address the challenges mentioned in the previous sections. The following subsection summarizes implications of the study, and the section ends with a discussion of issues for further research.

Shared Characteristics Among Outreach Programs Suggest Recipe for Success

All these programs shared a common record, by some measures, of success. All were able to perform effectively and to create a funding and support base to ensure their continued operation. In short, the participants we interviewed perceived the programs to be both sustainable and effective. In this subsection, we discuss the common characteristics of the outreach programs that contributed to their success, which include shared vision, personnel, strategic planning, support infrastructure, and locality.

Shared Vision

Outreach programs require an extraordinary amount of support and dedication from program participants. Conversations with program directors, coordinators, and managers indicated that a critical part of gaining this dedication is a shared vision of the importance of the outreach program. The vision is important because it serves to inspire and unite program participants from diverse backgrounds. For many of the outreach programs we visited, linking efforts to improve science education to a larger societal aim was critical. For example, some viewed improving science education in underserved communities as being a way to contribute to efforts to achieve social justice, and it was this vision of social justice that created the need to improve science education. Similarly for other programs, a vision of a university that is not disconnected from the ills of society surrounding them, but is instead committed to using the resources in the universities for change provided the basis for developing an outreach program focused on improving science education. It was important that this vision was broad enough so that others outside of the scientific and educational communities could rally around it and provide support. Shared vision was a critical component for overcoming challenges related to lack of buy-in from university faculty, deans, and other administrative officials.

Personnel

Frequently, the success of many of these programs was described as the result of the "sheer will" of extremely passionate people. In our interviews, phrases like "This program would not happen if not for Dr. X" or "the success of this program is due to X" were common. Many interviewees stated that programs and efforts like this could not be replicated without the involvement of certain key individuals. In fact, the term *magicians* was used to describe these all-important individuals who were able to make things happen seemingly out of thin air. Each program had a magician, and we were able to identify similar characteristics among these individuals that made them stand out. Typically, these individuals were

- senior faculty
- familiar with the intricacies of the university system and understood how it worked
- viewed as eminent in their discipline
- not concerned with maintaining the status quo.

This list does not imply that individuals without these characteristics cannot contribute to a successful program, but the consistency of these four characteristics across all the outreach programs we visited underscores their importance. The first feature, seniority, is a key element in leading outreach programs. One program director suggested that junior faculty would be ill-advised to try to run an outreach program:

> You have to get yourself established as to why you were hired in the first place. To put an assistant professor on a very prestigious or important academic committee with a heavy workload would be a disservice to the person and to the committee.

The importance of understanding the university system and how it works is important in gaining university support for these programs. Understanding the proper channels to go through can help increase the visibility of these programs to influential people. Having credibility and respect among one's peers is an important element in eliciting support from other faculty and high-level personnel. As suggested in the earlier quote, establishing oneself as a credible researcher is critical. All these attributes are important for the last characteristic listed. Lack of concern with maintaining the status quo tends to give these leaders a "trailblazer" persona and is absolutely essential for real reform. Too often, outreach programs devolve into "feel-good" programs that do no harm but also little good. A willingness to go beyond feel good attempts at outreach is important for programs like this to be successful. As one program director stated, "Any program like this always requires somebody who is willing to say 'I want this to happen and I will see to it that it does happen.'"

Along with strong leadership, it is also important to have productive partnerships. Although the "trailblazer" may be successful in the higher-education culture, he/she may not be well-suited for the negotiations that take place in school districts. Within many of these programs, we identified a partnership between a senior program director and a community liaison. The community liaison is generally a person who is part of the university but has had experience in the K–12 world that gives him/her the insight necessary to be effective in dealing with schools and districts.

Strategic Planning

Perhaps the most critical aspect in the success of many of these programs was having the time and resources necessary for strategic planning. Most programs were initially supported on small budgets, with a few dollars here and there, but with lots of freedom and flexibility for strategic planning. Most program directors felt that by, starting off small, they had the ability to construct the programs they way they wanted to, without having to deal with "the strings that are often attached" to federal or private funding. This also meant they had the time to select the appropriate personnel and build a solid base of trust between the university and the schools that they were working with. For those whose programs were initiated with federal funding, the urgency to get things going often meant that planning was more reactive than strategic. Many program directors felt that, if there had been one factor that could have improved the program, it would have been more time for planning.

Support Infrastructure

Seeking support from a wide range of participants is important in tapping into different resources. Frequently, these resources can be found in other university departments. For example, many sociology, psychology, and ethnic studies departments have also participated in different forms of outreach and can offer comments and suggestions about making inroads into district communities. Partnerships with schools of education are perhaps the most critical support resource to develop. Responsible for preparing future generations of teachers, schools of education offer a natural way to connect the science content with the pedagogical training. More than that, partnerships with schools of education give outreach programs a measure of credibility because they represent a potential investment in the community. Districts often view the transient nature of the outreach programs utilizing university students negatively; however, many schools viewed the presence of science graduate students partnered with preservice interns in their schools as a potential long-term investment.

Locality

Outreach programs where the universities were situated near or in the community with the partnering K–12 schools shared a common bond based on proximity. Problems and issues within the community affected both the university and the K–12 schools, and this created a much stronger bond between them. Moreover, the convenience of being able to walk to the schools should not be underestimated. Other programs that were located away from the schools they partnered with found that transportation issues created quite a hurdle.

Implications of Study

This research was designed to spotlight a small subset of programs and raise issues for further exploration. Thus, before any policy recommendations can be made, future research aimed at verifying and validating the results of this study must be done. However, we believe that a number of important issues emerged from this study. One of the major ideas is an understanding of the different ways outreach programs impact student learning. Improving student learning in science and math requires different things in different classrooms, for different students. A single outreach program cannot provide all of the resources needed to improve science and math learning in K–12 classrooms. However, good outreach programs can support classrooms and provide the necessary infrastructure to ensure that, while schools are in the process of change, student learning in science and math is not compromised. As schools work on developing more-rigorous science and math curriculums, attracting and retaining teachers with strong backgrounds in math and science, and creating instructional activities aimed at engaging students of all backgrounds, science graduate and undergraduate students can serve as an important tool to aid and expedite that process.

Another idea that emerged from the study is an awareness of the impact of high-stakes testing in math and reading on science instruction. At a time when the

National Science Education Standards are demanding that teachers develop a set of sophisticated and complex skills for teaching science, the amount of the time that classrooms spend on science instruction may be limited as a result of the emphasis on high-stakes testing. Our interviews suggested that these conflicting goals create a number of challenges for teachers, and in this environment, outreach programs that utilize university students may be an appropriate and much-needed resource to help resolve this tension.

This study also suggested that, to be successful, outreach programs must negotiate the barriers and obstacles present in both K–12 schools and institutions of higher education. Figure 5.1 provides a schematic diagram of these two cultures and illustrates some of the challenges within each culture. As shown, university science students represent the input from higher education being utilized to support teachers in their efforts to improve science learning in K–12 classrooms. As such, universities are responsible for both the quantity and quality of the science undergraduate and graduate students on which these programs depend. Thus, the support of institutions of higher education is critical to the success of these programs. It is difficult for outreach programs to be either sustainable or effective without a steady supply of qualified science students.

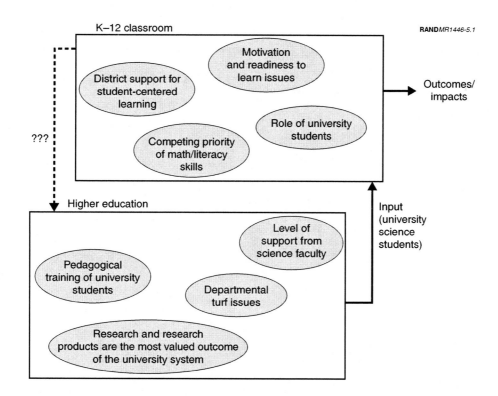

Figure 5.1—A Systems View of Outreach Programs

The four nodes within the higher-education box represent the challenges that were discussed in Section 4. While all these challenges potentially impact the input, the most critical is perhaps the emphasis on research and research products at most universities. One could argue that this emphasis in fact drives the creation of the other challenges. Consequently, getting and maintaining support from the university is an important objective for outreach programs. Without university support, few programs can be sustained for long; eventually, a lack of support will undermine their effectiveness in K–12 classrooms. This lack of support from science faculty, the lack of emphasis on the importance of developing good teaching skills, and potential concerns about increasing the time it takes for graduate students to obtain their doctoral degrees are all factors that affect the future recruitment and participation of graduate students and, to a lesser extent, undergraduate students.

On entering the K–12 school culture, university science students confront a number of challenges that affect their ability to support teachers' efforts to improve science learning. The nodes in the box labeled "K–12 classrooms" highlight many of the challenges discussed in Section 3. While challenges in the higher-education culture essentially stem from an emphasis on research, the challenges in the K–12 world are quite divergent, and the factors that create and influence them vary tremendously. For example, increasing district support for outreach programs may increase the focus on student-centered learning; however, other issues, such as motivation to learn and the emphasis on math and literacy skills, still to challenge the effectiveness of these programs.

Ironically, the net effect of the challenges in both cultures is the same: Science education is being squeezed out and given less attention. Both cultures have a number of obstacles to emphasizing and teaching science in a meaningful way. In the K–12 world, the competing priority of high-stakes testing in math and reading often contributes to the lack of attention to science education. In the higher-education culture, the emphasis on research can often result in the devaluation of science teaching and education in the university system.

This study also raises the issue of incentives for the participation of universities in outreach programs. The dashed arrow in Figure 5.1 indicates that there is a critical feedback loop from K–12 schools to the institution of higher education that needs further development. The study suggests that creating incentives for universities to participate in outreach is critical to the sustainability of these programs, and program directors and coordinators should pay attention to the unique attributes of the partnerships between universities and K–12 schools. Certainly, one area worth pursuing is the in-depth learning that many graduate students reported as a result of interacting with K–12 teachers and students.

Community support for the universities is another important benefit, especially to universities located near the K–12 schools they partner with. Moreover, universities might consider using faculty research (when appropriate) as a method of supplementing K–12 curriculum materials. Not only would this provide K–12 students with customized and modern science topics for discussion, it could also be used as a basis for getting more "buy-in" from the science faculty.

Issues for Future Study

This study suggests several areas of research that deserve further attention, including areas include program design, evaluation, and implementation issues. Building on the ideas presented in Figure 5.1, the schematic in Figure 5.2 illustrates where these issues are located. For example, a number of program-design issues emerge from the links between the higher-education culture and the K–12 classrooms; implementation issues emerge from the challenges that

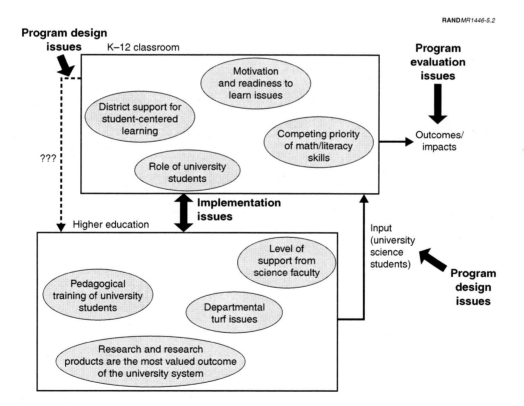

Figure 5.2—Program Design, Evaluation, and Implementation
Issues in Outreach Programs

program participants identified; and evaluation issues are embedded in the discussion on the outcomes and impacts of these programs.

Program Design Issues

Targeting the needs of the K–12 schools in the most appropriate and effective manner is an important issue in program design. The programs that we have discussed in this report represent a spectrum of different intervention efforts that range from those that require little classroom contact (e.g., remote classroom enhancement programs) to the those that involve more sustained classroom interaction (e.g., direct classroom enhancement). Thus, one strategy for targeting school needs effectively would be to develop a university-based program that contains a portfolio of different intervention approaches for partnering the talents and skills of university students with K–12 classrooms. This would allow outreach programs more flexibility in coordinating their efforts with K–12 schools. For example, rather than starting out with direct enhancement programs, K–12 schools and universities might elect to begin working together through remote enhancement programs in which graduate students interact via the Internet. If more support is needed over time, the trust and camaraderie that have been built from a nonintrusive method of support can be used to "smooth the way" in developing more-intensive methods of outreach. Combining efforts under a single program would also allow program directors to focus on developing effective ways to utilize the talents of university science students.

Although having graduate students available via e-mail may represent a "drop in the reform bucket" for some schools, this intervention may be all that is needed for some classroom teachers to become more confident and creative in their science instruction. However, if more-intensive efforts are needed, such as placing students in classrooms, these programs could use the infrastructure that has been developed for less intensive efforts to create more extensive networks with K–12 schools and could prepare graduate students to enter into K–12 classrooms with sound training in science education. These programs could also research and explore alternative design strategies utilizing graduate and undergraduate students. Graduate students *are* an expensive intervention, and strategies that mix undergraduate students, and preservice teachers may create cost-effective, as well as pedagogically sound, ways of increasing the impact of university students visiting schools.

These programs could also begin to create pathways that address the need to bring students with strong science and math backgrounds into teaching professions. Subject-matter knowledge is important in teaching because it affects the confidence that teachers bring to the subjects they teach and their ability to be creative in developing curriculum. Because many of these programs focus on recruiting students with aptitude in science and math, they may offer a way to channel students into teaching careers.

This study also suggests that program design should build in more incentives for the universities. A number of ideas were mentioned in Section 4, and further research could be done to identify which incentives would be most beneficial to universities.

Evaluation Issues

Clearly, the issue of evaluation needs to be dealt with. A better understanding is needed of what it is these programs are actually doing. Program directors explained to us that the project budgets do not provide for rigorous evaluation efforts. Consequently, evaluation strategies are not part of the original project designs. Moreover, because outreach programs are often part of larger science research grants, the effectiveness of the education outreach component has little impact on continued or renewed grant support. While many of the programs we visited had some form of evaluation, most of the evaluations were designed to improve various features of the program rather than to determine how well the program was achieving its stated goals and objectives. Evaluation is a critical part of the success of these programs, and stronger incentives for high-quality and continuous evaluation need to be created. Although looking at student achievement in math and science is important, these evaluations should be sensitive to the multidimensional aspects of the programs and should be geared to detect what these programs are doing, such as increasing student motivation and enthusiasm for science, increasing teacher collegiality, changing teacher practices, and changing teacher attitudes toward science. As stated in Section 3, one of the primary contributions of the science students was their ability to facilitate immediate changes in teacher attitudes and teaching practices. If these programs are viewed in light of *facilitating* change rather than *producing* change, the metrics should focus on measuring the changes in classroom conditions and school environments.

Moreover, the evaluations should also measure impacts on the higher-education side. Improved communication in science, increased enrollment in science courses as a result of adding an outreach component to traditional science classes, and a deeper awareness and understanding of societal issues were all mentioned as important impacts in this study, and future research should focus on how to measure these impacts. Strong evaluations that measure impacts on both the K–12 classroom and the university science students could move these outreach activities from peripheral programs to integral components of the university because they would be viewed as having measurable positive impacts on the graduate students that participate in them, as well as on the K–12 students and teachers.

Implementation Issues

Many of the major implementation issues are centered on the personal relationship between the universities and the schools. Getting buy-in from schools and districts for outreach programs hinges on building mutual trust and respect between universities and schools. Developing trust takes time. For some programs, one year is all that is needed to make connections and build relationships; for others, it may take longer. And yet, the foundation for successful implementation depends on this key ingredient. Many interviewees stated that a lack of time created a number of implementation challenges early in the process. Building a planning period into the structure of the sponsoring grant may be one way to address this issue and was suggested by a number of program participants.

Other implementation issues stem from disjointed efforts among program participants, and having a single coordinated effort is crucial. As one program director described,

> Although any one of us individually could step out into the surrounding area, into the schools, we would run into various brick walls, social context, political context, and there are all sorts of things you don't understand. At some point you are all on the same side, you want students to learn science and math better, but there's all this subtext, and the coordinated effort helps people get around that.

Programs that were able to coordinate their efforts through community partnerships were able to be much more effective in connecting to K–12 classrooms and building sustainable long-term relationships.

This study also suggests that the characteristics of the university culture are critical to implementation and should be considered carefully. Universities with a strong emphasis on research present a number of implementation challenges. Program directors should consider universities whose missions encompass many of the goals of the outreach programs. State-supported colleges and/or historically minority universities with long histories of community outreach may have stronger incentives to participate in outreach programs, as well as an infrastructure that more easily accommodates partnerships with K–12 schools.

Finally, this study suggests that implementing outreach programs that involve science university students is inherently difficult. Therefore, supporting and expanding existing partnerships (with a set of "successful" characteristics) may be more cost-effective than creating new programs.

Appendix

A. Interview Protocols

This appendix contains the interview protocol we used on our site visits to universities and K–12 schools. We used the teacher interview protocol for K–12 classroom teachers we interviewed. The scientist interview protocol was used for interviews with undergraduate and graduate students. For interviews with program directors, coordinators and managers, we used the program administrator interview protocol.

Teacher Interview Protocol

Q1:   To get things started, let's go around the room. I'd like a brief explanation of what led to your participation in the XXX program.

    P1:   Were there any incentives (explicit or implicit) provided?

Q2:   Do you feel that you benefit from your participation in the program?

    P1:   If so, how?

Q3:   Has your experience in this program changed your classroom teaching?

    P1:   If so, how?

    P2:   As a result of this program, what sorts of things will you emphasize in your classroom teaching of science?

Q4:   Based on your experience, what are the goals and objectives of this program?

Q5:   Did you find interacting with the scientists useful?

    P1:   If so, what aspect did you feel was most useful in terms of your interactions with the scientists?

Q6:   Did you feel comfortable interacting with the scientists?

    P1:   Did you have any challenges or difficulties working with the scientists?

    P2:   Have you had direct interactions with the faculty? Based on your experience do find working with graduate and undergraduate students to be suitable?

    P3:   Why or why not?

Q7: Do you expect to be able to sustain the benefits from your participation in this program?

P1: If so, how?

P2: Would it be helpful to have more frequent workshops or interactions?

Q8: Just some background questions:

P1: What grade level do you teach?

P2: How much science background have you had?

Q9: Based on your experience, does this program enhance science learning on the part of the students?

P1: If so, how?

Q10: What is your overall assessment of the program?

P1: What are some of the features you consider to be critical to the success of this program?

P2: What do you consider to be some of the shortcomings of this program?

P3: What changes would you like to make to the program and why?

Scientist Interview Protocol

Q1:   To get things started, let's go around the room. I'd like to get a brief explanation of what led to your participation in program XXX.

     P1:   Were there any incentives (explicit or implicit) provided?

Q2:   Do you feel that you benefit from your participation in the program?

     P1:   If so, how?

Q3:   Have you had prior teaching experience?

     P1:   If so, did you find the experience of working in the classrooms to be different?

     P2:   If so, how?

Q4:   Did you find there to be any unique challenges or difficulties in working in the classrooms?

     P1:   If so, what were they?

     P2:   What sort of adjustments did you have to make?

Q5:   Based on your experience, what are the goals and objectives of this program?

Q6:   What sort of scientific principles or ideas did you try to emphasize in your interactions in the classroom?

Q7:   Did you feel comfortable interacting with the teachers?

     P1:   Why or why not?

Q8:   What is your overall assessment of the program?

     P1:   What do you consider to be the strengths of this program?

     P2:   What do you consider to be some of the shortcomings of this program?

     P3:   What changes would you like to make to the program and why?

Program Administrator Interview Protocol

Q1: I'd like to understand how the program works. Tell me a little bit about the program. For example:

    P1: What selection process do you use for the teachers?

    P2: Are there any particular groups of teachers that you have targeted?

    P3: For the scientists?

    P4: How do you match the teacher with the scientist?

Q2: What are the goals and objectives of the program?

Q3: What was the underlying motivation for the program?

Q4: What led you to create and implement the program?

Q5: Do you feel that this program enhances science teaching?

    P1: If so, how?

Q6: Do you feel that this program enhances science learning on the part of the students?

    P1: If so, how?

Q7: How long has the program been in operation?

Q8: How many teachers and scientists are normally involved in the program?

    P1: Has this changed over time?

Q9: What were some of the challenges you faced in setting up this program?

Q10: I would be interested in your overall assessment of the program.

    P1: What do you consider to be the strengths of this program?

    P2: What do you consider to be some of the shortcomings of this program?

    P3: What changes would you like to make to the program and why?

    P4: Do you have plans to make any changes to the program?

Q11: Are you conducting or planning any kind of an evaluation of the program?

    P1: For example, do you survey your teachers and scientists to get their reactions and comments?

B. Program Characteristics

This appendix provides information about each of the outreach programs we visited. The information for each program was obtained from interview data, program materials that were given to us, and Web site information.

Direct Classroom Enhancement Programs

PROGRAM NAME: DCE1

PROGRAM DESCRIPTION: This program brings graduate and undergraduate teaching fellows together with research scientists and in-service and preservice teachers to help improve mathematics, science, and technology education for students in K–12 school classrooms.

PROGRAM GOALS AND OBJECTIVES: Bringing science content into K–12 classroom while improving undergraduate and graduate education at the university

PROGRAM APPROACH: Direct classroom enhancement

PROGRAM FUNDING SOURCE: NSF

PROGRAM EVALUATION: None yet[1]

SCOPE OF IMPACT: 6 public schools[2]

GRADE LEVEL: K–12

SCHOOL PROFILE: >88 percent African-American students; more than 86 percent of the pupils are from low income families; all schools have Chapter I eligibility

PROGRAM DURATION: Academic school year and summer

SCHOOL COMMUNITY: Urban

SCIENTIFIC DISCIPLINE[3]: Life sciences, physical sciences, engineering and mathematics

CARNEGIE CLASSIFICATION OF SPONSORING UNIVERSITY: Research I

NUMBER OF PARTICIPATING SCIENTISTS: 7 graduate and 17 undergraduate fellows

AMOUNT OF TIME SCIENTISTS INVOLVED IN OUTREACH: 15–20 hrs/week

COMPENSATION FOR SCIENTISTS' TIME: Stipend

---

[1] This information is based on the response to question 11 in the Program Administrator interview protocol.

[2] Information about the exact number of teachers and students participating in this programs was unavailable at the time of interview).

[3] Scientific discipline refers to the backgrounds of the scientists that participated in the outreach program.

PROGRAM NAME: DCE2

PROGRAM DESCRIPTION: Teachers are supported 3–4 hours per week by science undergraduates. The undergraduates are trained at their institutions in the inquiry approach to learning science.

PROGRAM GOALS AND OBJECTIVES: Systemic conversion of elementary science education to an inquiry-centered, constructivist approach through the use of kit-based modules and the provision of appropriate professional development—and classroom support—for teachers

PROGRAM APPROACH: Direct classroom enhancement, teacher professional development, instructional materials development[4]

PROGRAM FUNDING SOURCE: NSF

PROGRAM EVALUATION: Yes

SCOPE OF IMPACT: 68 elementary (K–5) schools; 1,700 teachers and 35,000 students

GRADE LEVEL: K–5

SCHOOL PROFILE: >92 percent African-American students; over 82 percent of all students eligible for reduced lunches

PROGRAM DURATION: Academic school year

SCHOOL COMMUNITY: Urban

SCIENTIFIC DISCIPLINE: Life sciences, earth sciences

CARNEGIE CLASSIFICATION OF SPONSORING UNIVERSITY: Research I

NUMBER OF PARTICIPATING SCIENTISTS: 175 undergraduates

AMOUNT OF TIME SCIENTISTS INVOLVED IN OUTREACH: 3–4 hrs/week in classroom

COMPENSATION FOR SCIENTISTS' TIME: University credit hours

---

[4]Although primarily a direct classroom enhancement program, this program also included other components in its outreach activities as well.

PROGRAM NAME: DCE3

PROGRAM DESCRIPTION: Teams of medical, nursing, and public health students are recruited and trained to work with school personnel to help introduce heath-science concepts; assist with in-school, after-school, and summer enrichment activities; provide support and serve as agents of change

PROGRAM GOALS AND OBJECTIVES: Encourage K–12 students to think scientifically about health concerns and health decisions

PROGRAM APPROACH: Direct classroom support, teacher professional development

PROGRAM FUNDING SOURCE: NIH

PROGRAM EVALUATION: Teachers complete forms to evaluate progress at local schools

SCOPE OF IMPACT: 6 middle schools, over 300 students

GRADE LEVEL: 6–8

SCHOOL PROFILE: >92 percent African-American students; over 82 percent of all students eligible for reduced lunches

PROGRAM DURATION: Academic school year

SCHOOL COMMUNITY : Urban

SCIENTIFIC DISCIPLINE: Health sciences

CARNEGIE CLASSIFICATION OF SPONSORING UNIVERSITY: Research I

NUMBER OF PARTICIPATING SCIENTISTS: 43 graduate students

AMOUNT OF TIME SCIENTISTS INVOLVED IN OUTREACH: Minimum of 6 hrs/month

COMPENSATION FOR SCIENTISTS' TIME: Stipend

PROGRAM NAME: TP1

PROGRAM DESCRIPTION: This program provides math and science majors a full year of intense observation and participation in urban school classrooms during their senior year and appropriate education courses during that year and the following summer. The fifth year (graduate level) consists of a full year's teaching experience under an emergency teaching credential.

PROGRAM GOALS AND OBJECTIVES: Interest prospective undergraduate mathematics and science majors in a school teaching career

PROGRAM APPROACH: Teacher preparation

PROGRAM FUNDING SOURCE: University supported program

PROGRAM EVALUATION: State evaluation, surveys, and questionnaires at the end of the program on course-level (at the end of the quarter) and program-level state credentialing units as well as the university academic unit; students evaluate the program at the end of the course; an ongoing inquiry session is also used for evaluation

SCOPE OF IMPACT: Averages about 13 students per year matriculating through teacher-preparation program; so far, has placed over 100 hundred math majors in schools

GRADE LEVEL: Secondary and high school

SCHOOL PROFILE: Either (1) at least 50 percent of the school's students receive free or reduced lunch, and no one racial group constitutes more than 50 percent of the total student body, **or** (2) the school's student body is majority Latino, African American, or Asian

PROGRAM DURATION: Academic school year

SCHOOL COMMUNITY: Urban

SCIENTIFIC DISCIPLINE: Mathematics and science (biology, chemistry, and physics)

CARNEGIE CLASSIFICATION OF SPONSORING UNIVERSITY: Research I

NUMBER OF PARTICIPATING SCIENTISTS: 13 undergraduates

AMOUNT OF TIME SCIENTISTS INVOLVED IN OUTREACH: 5 hrs of classroom participation per week

COMPENSATION FOR SCIENTISTS' TIME: Stipend, teaching certification

Teacher-Researcher Programs

PROGRAM NAME: TR1

PROGRAM DESCRIPTION: Teachers work with science graduate students in a research laboratory to learn about laboratory research and current topics and techniques in biology. In addition to the research experience, participating teachers also have ongoing access to a science-kit loan program with technical support.

PROGRAM GOALS AND OBJECTIVES: Provide productive interaction between individual science teachers and scientists in a setting that provides hands-on experimentation and resource development; establish long-term partnerships between teachers and the scientific research community; and increase scientists' ability to communicate science

PROGRAM APPROACH: Teacher professional development, instructional materials development

PROGRAM FUNDING SOURCE: Howard Hughes Medical Institute and research center support

PROGRAM EVALUATION: Formal outside evaluation, part of collaborative multisite study to measure the impact teacher-researcher programs have on students

SCOPE OF IMPACT: 25 teachers per summer, directly influences approximately 3, 750 students annually, currently over 11,000 students use kits

GRADE LEVEL: Middle school or junior high; high school (5th–12th)

SCHOOL PROFILE: 77.5 percent white, 2.7 percent Native-American, 6.7 percent Asian, 4.8 percent African-American, 8.3 percent Hispanic[5]

PROGRAM DURATION: 2.5 weeks during summer; graduate students provide ongoing support throughout the academic year

SCHOOL COMMUNITY : Suburban, rural, and urban

SCIENTIFIC DISCIPLINE: Molecular biology and genetics

CARNEGIE CLASSIFICATION OF SPONSORING UNIVERSITY: Research I

NUMBER OF PARTICIPATING SCIENTISTS: Currently 8 graduate students

AMOUNT OF TIME SCIENTISTS INVOLVED IN OUTREACH: Varies, in place of teaching assistantship

COMPENSATION FOR SCIENTISTS' TIME: Graduate students get TA credit

---

[5]Based on average from 1997–1998 state enrollment.

PROGRAM NAME: TR2

PROGRAM DESCRIPTION: This program engages secondary science teachers in laboratory research and in the creation of innovative interactive curricular materials and discovery-based projects.

PROGRAM GOALS AND OBJECTIVES: Teachers will gain experience in the scientific experimentation process and collaborate to translate investigative science activities into their classrooms.

PROGRAM APPROACH: Teacher professional development

PROGRAM FUNDING SOURCE: NSF

PROGRAM EVALUATION: Before and after surveys of teacher and mentor scientist participants; academic year meeting to prepare spring workshop for fellow teachers to disseminate new curriculum

SCOPE OF IMPACT: 6 teachers per summer

GRADE LEVEL: Middle and high schools

SCHOOL PROFILE:

PROGRAM DURATION: 2-year cycle that includes two summer workshops (1st summer, 6-week workshop; 2nd summer, 4-week workshop) and monthly meetings during two academic years

SCHOOL COMMUNITY: Suburban and rural

SCIENTIFIC DISCIPLINE: Material sciences

CARNEGIE CLASSIFICATION OF SPONSORING UNIVERSITY: Research I

NUMBER OF PARTICIPATING SCIENTISTS: 6 scientists per year

AMOUNT OF TIME SCIENTISTS INVOLVED IN OUTREACH: Varies depending on research project

COMPENSATION FOR SCIENTISTS' TIME: None—voluntary

Remote Classroom Enhancement Program

PROGRAM NAME: RC1

PROGRAM DESCRIPTION: This Internet-based program enriches science instruction by fostering interactions between K–12 students and teachers and university scientists via e-mail. Teachers and K–12 students send questions about any area of science to scientists at the university, and university science students provide detailed explanations and answers.

PROGRAM GOALS AND OBJECTIVES: Connecting university scientists to local community schools, providing easy and convenient accessibility to content knowledge of scientists

PROGRAM APPROACH: Remote classroom enhancement

PROGRAM FUNDING SOURCE: NSF and university grant

PROGRAM EVALUATION: Archive of all questions asked and feedback from participating teachers

SCOPE OF IMPACT: 11 teachers (3 elementary, 6 junior high, and 2 high school teachers)

GRADE LEVEL: Elementary, junior high, and high school

SCHOOL PROFILE: Students are from nearby ranches and farms; local economy is based on agriculture; many of the students come from migrant families; student population is ethnically mixed, with 90 percent Hispanic, 4 percent Filipino, 3 percent white, 1 percent black, 2 percent other

PROGRAM DURATION: Academic school year

SCHOOL COMMUNITY: Rural, migrant community

SCIENTIFIC DISCIPLINE: Life sciences, earth sciences, and physical sciences

CARNEGIE CLASSIFICATION OF SPONSORING UNIVERSITY: Research I university

NUMBER OF PARTICIPATING SCIENTISTS: 3–4 undergrad, 12 graduate students, and a few postdocs

AMOUNT OF TIME SCIENTISTS INVOLVED IN OUTREACH: Varies depending on number of questions and level of detail in scientific explanation

COMPENSATION FOR SCIENTISTS' TIME: None—voluntary

Instructional Materials Development Program

PROGRAM NAME: IMD1

PROGRAM DESCRIPTION: Undergraduate students design, build, and maintain instructional materials for science classroom instruction.

PROGRAM GOALS AND OBJECTIVES: Provides hands-on resources for classroom use to introduce students and teachers to the science behind computers and fiber-optics technology

PROGRAM APPROACH: Development of instructional materials, direct classroom support, professional development for teachers

PROGRAM FUNDING SOURCE: Initially NSF; currently supported with private foundation funding and university funding

PROGRAM EVALUATION: Teacher surveys

SCOPE OF IMPACT: 3,500 students

GRADE LEVEL: 5th–12th grades

SCHOOL PROFILE: 80 percent Latino (agricultural community); 40 percent of students below poverty level

PROGRAM DURATION: Academic school year

SCHOOL COMMUNITY: Rural, migrant community

SCIENTIFIC DISCIPLINE: Physical sciences, engineering

CARNEGIE CLASSIFICATION OF SPONSORING UNIVERSITY: Research I University

NUMBER OF PARTICIPATING SCIENTISTS : 6 undergraduates and 2 faculty

AMOUNT OF TIME SCIENTISTS INVOLVED IN OUTREACH: 10 hrs/week for undergraduates and 10/hrs month for faculty

COMPENSATION FOR SCIENTISTS' TIME: Stipend

Bibliography

American Association for the Advancement of Science, *Benchmarks for Science Literacy*, New York: Oxford University Press, 1993.

_____, *Science for All Americans*, New York: Oxford University Press, 1989.

Alberts, Bruce, and Karen Worth, eds., *Resources for Scientists Involved in Pre-College Science Education*, Bethesda Md.: The American Society for Cell Biology and Washington, D.C.: The Education Development Center, Inc., 1991.

Anderson, Charles W., "Reform in Teacher Education as Building Systemic Capacity to Support the Scholarship of Teaching," in Kathy Comfort, ed., *Advancing Standards for Science and Mathematics Education: Views from the Field*, Washington, D.C.: American Association for the Advancement of Science, 1999. Online at http://www.Ehrweb.aaas.org.ehr.forum.Andersn.html (as of March 12, 2002).

Bacon, W. Stevenson, ed., *Bringing the Excitement of Science to the Classroom*, Tucson, Ariz.: Research Corporation, 2000.

Bredderman, T., "Effects of Activity-Based Elementary Science on Student Outcomes: A Quantitative Synthesis," *Review of Educational Research*, Vol. 53, No. 4, 1983.

Clune, William H., Deborah Tepper Haimo, Judy Roitman, Thomas Romberg, John C. Wright, and Carol S. Wright, *Commentaries on Mathematics and Science Standards*, Madison, Wisc.: National Institute for Science Education, Occasional Paper No. 3, 1997.

Dow, Peter, *Schoolhouse Politics: Lessons from the Sputnik Era*, Cambridge, Mass.: Harvard University Press, 1991.

Gómez, Manuel, *"A K–16+ Continuum to Achieve Academic Excellence,"* presented at the Gordon Research Conference: New Frontiers in Science and Technology Policy, Plymouth, N.H., August 23, 2000.

Grissmer, David, Ann Flanagan, Jennifer Kawata, and Stephanie Williamson, *Improving Student Achievement: What State NAEP Test Scores Tell Us*, Santa Monica, Calif.: RAND, MR-924-EDU, 2000.

Haase, David G., and Brenda S. Wojnowski, eds., *Proceedings of the Conference on K–12 Outreach from University Science Departments*, held at North Carolina State University, Raleigh, N.C., February 10–12, 2000.

Kahle, Jane B., *"Measuring Progress Toward Equity in Science and Mathematics Education,"* Madison, Wisc.: National Institute of Science Education, 1998.

Moreno, Nancy P., "K–12 Science Education Reform—A Primer for Scientists," *Bioscience*, Vol. 49, No. 7, July 1999.

National Research Council, *Fulfilling the Promise, Biology Education in the Nation's Schools*, Washington D.C.: National Academy Press, 1990

_____, *National Science Education Standards*, Washington, D.C.: National Academy Press, 1996.

National Science Foundation, *The SSIs' Impacts on Classroom Practice*, Menlo Park, Calif.: SRI International, 1998.

National Science Foundation, Directorate for Education and Human Resources, *Evaluation of the National Science Foundation's Statewide Systemic Initiatives (SSI) Program: Second Year Report*, Arlington, Va., 1995.

National Science Resource Center, National Academy of Sciences, and Smithsonian Institution, *Science for All Children: A Guide to Improving Elementary Science Education in Your District*, Washington D.C.: National Academy Press, 1997.

NCES—*See* U.S. Department of Education, National Center for Educational Statistics.

NCMS—*See* U.S. Department of Education, National Commission on Mathematics and Science.

NSF—*See* National Science Foundation.

Noguera, Pedro A., "Toward the Development of School and University Partnerships Based Upon Mutual Benefit and Respect," *In Motion Magazine*, 2000. Online at http://www.inmotionmagazine.com/pnsup1.html (as of March 21, 2002).

Ogburn, Jon, Gunther Kress, Isabel Martins, and Kieran McGillicuddy, *Explaining Science in the Classroom*, Buckingham, England: Open University Press, 1996.

Popper, Steven W., Caroline S. Wagner, and Eric V. Larson, *New Forces at Work: Industry Views Critical Technologies*, Santa Monica, Calif.: RAND, MR-1008-OSTP, 1998.

Pritchard, Ivor, *Judging Standards in Standards-Based Reform*, Washington, D.C.: Council for Basic Education, 1996.

Raizen, S., *Standards for Science Education*, Madison, Wisc.: National Institute of Science Education, Occasional Paper No. 1, 1997.

Rubin, Herbert J., and Rubin, Irene S., *Qualitative Interviewing: The Art of Hearing Data*, Thousand Oaks, Calif.: Sage Publications, 1995.

Sandia National Laboratories, *Science Education in Our Elementary and Secondary Schools: A Guide for Technical Professions Who Want to Help*, brochure, Albuquerque, N.M., undated.

Schmidt, William H., Curtis C. McKnight, Leland S. Cogan, Pamela M. Jakworth, and Richard T. Houang, *Facing the Consequences,* Norwell, Mass.: Kluwer Academic Publishers, 1999.

Shymanky, J. A., "What Research Says About ESS, SCIS, and SAPA," *Science and Children,* Vol. 26, No. 7, 1989, pp. 33–35.

Stewart, David, W. and Shamdasani, Prem N., *Focus Groups: Theory and Practice,* Newbury Park, Calif.: Sage Publications, 1990.

Timpane, P. Michael and Lori S. White, eds., *Higher Education and School Reform,* San Francisco, Calif.: Jossey-Bass Inc., 1998.

U.S. Department of Education, National Center for Educational Statistics, *NAEP 1996 Trends in Academic Progress, Washington,* D.C.: U.S. Government Printing Office, NCES 97-985, 1997.

U.S. Department of Education, National Commission on Mathematics and Science, *Before It's Too Late: A Report to the Nation from The National Commission on Mathematics and Science Teaching for the 21st Century,* Washington, D.C., 2000.

Whitaker, Thomas R., "On Common Ground: Science, Technology and Teaching," *On Common Ground: Partnerships in Science and Technology,* No. 4, Spring 1995. Online at http://www.cls.yale.edu/ynhti/pubs/A17/ (as of March 21, 2002).